PELION

PHILIP E BARTOW

Copyright © 2014 Philip E Bartow

All rights reserved.

ISBN: 098351769X

ISBN 13: 9780983517696

CONTENTS

FOREWORD — v
PROLOGUE: **TESTIMONY TO COURAGE** — vii
PREFACE — ix

CHAPTER

1 **JUNE 21, 1981** — 1
2 **JUNE 22: TRAINING, DAY 1** — 27
3 **JUNE 23: TRAINING, DAY 2** — 39
4 **JUNE 24: TRAINING, DAY 3** — 49
5 **JUNE 25: TRAINING, DAY 4** — 61
6 **JUNE 26: TRAINING, DAY 5** — 73
7 **JUNE 27, 28 ONWARD TO MT. RAINIER** — 81
8 **JUNE 29 MT. RAINIER, DAY 1** — 91
9 **JUNE 30 MT. RAINIER, DAY 2** — 111
10 **JULY 1, MT. RAINIER, DAY 3** — 121
11 **JULY 2, MT. RAINIER, DAY 4. HIGH CAMP** — 131
12 **JULY 3, MT. RAINIER, DAY 5, THE SUMMIT** — 141
13 **JULY 3, MT. RAINIER, DAY 5 AVALANCHE** — 157
14 **JULY 4, INDEPENDENCE DAY, PARADISE LODGE** — 161

EPILOG — 167

SINCE PELION — 175

BEFORE PELION — 183

FOREWORD

Eleven intelligent, reasonable men and women, with courage and a spirit of adventure, decided to climb Mount Rainier in the State of Washington. None had ever climbed a mountain before but they all wanted to see if they could do it.

Mt. Rainier is a glaciated, heavily crevassed and steep-ridged mountain that rises to 14,410 feet above the sea level of Puget Sound. Its challenge is such that half of those who try to reach the summit do not make it. Those who do make it say, "It's the hardest thing I've ever done."

When this group shouldered their packs and set foot on the climb, they also knew that eleven climbers had been killed in an icefall on the same route only one week earlier. With full knowledge, aware of the risk as well as the difficulty, each one decided to go ahead with the climb.

The team of unique individuals was the dream and reality of Phil Bartow, a mountaineer and humanitarian. Dianne and I were honored to be able to rope up with them.

PELION

They were seven blind, two deaf, one epileptic and the eleventh had an artificial leg. They are an inspiration to all of us.

Jim Whittaker

PROLOGUE

TESTIMONY TO COURAGE

PELION began as a climb for eleven people and ended as a statement for a nation.

It was a dream;
> Dark steps over unseen spaces,
> Movements in pain,
> Unheard calls of warning,
> Joy on a summit.

Pelion is a statement that disabilities are in the mind and incompleteness of the body only an inconvenience.

Pelion is testimony to the courage of all disabled persons who overcome their own mountains of despair in the spirit of those who climbed one of nature's majestic peaks.

PREFACE

PROJECT PELION: A team of disabled persons climbed to the 14,410-foot summit of Mount Rainier as an American contribution to the International Year of Disabled Persons in 1981. I thought of the idea for the project in October of 1979. This book describes the often tedious planning and the incredible adventure of the climb. It is a story about people who have done something that had not been done before. While there are other stories about individual blind climbers, this is the first account of an expedition by a team made up of blind members as well as people with other disabilities. It is a story about the deaf providing the eyes for the blind and the blind being the ears for the deaf. It was then and is now a much-needed uplifting story of the boundless capacity of the human spirit.

This is the story about a project that most people, including some of the participants, did not believe had a chance until it started. The climb is a statement that we will not know what will work until we try. It is a story about trying.

Project Pelion is a story about nature. The philosophy behind Pelion is that nature provides the basis for growth, for learning and for demonstration. What more graphic way to demonstrate human potential than to climb a mountain?

PELION

One reason for writing this account is to provide a record for the people with disabilities and for the therapists, counselors and others working with the disabled, that the living joy of adventure in life is possible. If when Judy Oehler lost her sight to diabetes in 1970 somebody had told her that she would climb mountains she would have had no reason to believe them. Now Judy has become a reason for others to believe. In fact, the myth of statistics would have given Judy only five years to live. That was almost ten years before Pelion.

The project reflects the spirit and philosophy behind the Institute For Outdoor Awareness. The project title, Pelion, is taken from Greek Mythology. The giant brothers Otus and Ephialtes were battling with the gods and wanted to get to the heavens. They piled Mt. Ossa on top of Mt. Olympus and then put Mt. Pelion on top of Mt. Ossa. Mt. Pelion was a stepping stone to the heavens.

Philip E. Bartow
Institute For Outdoor Awareness, Inc.

CHAPTER 1

JUNE 21, 1981

June 21, 1981 was the worst day in American mountaineering. On Mt. Rainier, just before sunrise, eleven climbers stopped at 12,000 feet for a rest before starting up the steep traverse under the icy cliffs of Disappointment Cleaver. As they sat in the pre-dawn twilight, tons of ice broke away from the glacier bordering the Cleaver above them. They were buried in the avalanche of ice blocks. Seventy-five miles to the south, in Oregon, five other climbers were killed in an avalanche of snow on Mt. Hood.

About the time the eleven were being swept to their deaths on Mount Rainier I was driving from Aspen to Denver to meet eleven people who were going to start training for a climb of Mount Rainier fourteen days later. The planned expedition would take them under the same fateful ice fall. The members of the team were flying into Denver from different parts of the country to rendezvous and drive to Aspen. Two were coming in from Seattle, one from Portland, Oregon, one from Kansas City, one from Boston, one from New York City, three from Philadelphia and two from Washington, D.C. They arrived on different flights over a period of three hours.

PELION

Richard Rose, from Portland, arrived first at 10:20. As we met there was a sense of challenge and adventure in starting something that had never been done before: venturing onto a renowned mountain to do something that many people did not think could be done.

The team was unique. The members were individuals who wanted to climb a mountain against the odds of a physical handicap. Seven of them were blind. No blind person had ever climbed Mt. Rainier. One of the blind was also diabetic. Two of the climbers were deaf, another was epileptic and the eleventh was an amputee. None of the eleven were mountaineers. Several had never carried a pack before. A couple of them had never been camping. Four, who had been blind since early childhood, really did not know what a mountain was.

The first eight to arrive were introduced to one another for the time and packed into Big Blue, a large Chevy carryall we borrowed from friends of Judy Oehler. Judy was one of the blind climbers and a key participant in the planning of the Pelion Project. While I waited for the later planes to arrive, Roy Fitzgerald (Fitz), a close friend and physician-member of the Board of the Institute for Outdoor Awareness and a specialist in working with the visually impaired, drove Big Blue to Aspen. We planned to meet at the St. Moritz Lodge in Aspen later in the afternoon. With Fitz were Sheila Holzworth, Judy Oehler, Chuck O'Brien, Richard Rose, Justin McDevitt, Fred Noesner, Bud Keith and Doug Wakefield. Sheila, Judy, Justin, Fred, Bud and Doug were totally blind. Richard had epilepsy and Chuck had lost a leg in Viet Nam.

JUNE 21, 1981

After Fitz departed I went to find Alec Naiman who was visiting his sister in Denver. Alec and his sister were both deaf. When I knocked on the door there was no response so I knocked harder. A neighbor said I would have to knock hard several times or call them. Eventually a lady opened the door and I explained I was looking for Alec. This was my first effort at trying to talk to a deaf person. She read my lips when I asked for Alec. She went into another room and came back with him. We introduced ourselves for the first time. He retrieved his backpack, said goodbye to his sister and we drove back to the airport.

By mid-afternoon Paul Stefurak and Kirk Adams arrived and were waiting at an information counter. I introduced them to each other and we headed for Aspen.

The three-hour drive from Denver to Aspen is spectacular. Leaving the flat valley of Denver, the highway follows along the bottom of steep canyons. Old mines dot the walls. For long uphill stretches the highway climbs to 9,000 feet, and then runs across the tops of mountains before descending into another steep canyon.

Alec and Paul, both deaf, were in the back seat and Kirk Adams sat up front. I watched Alec and Paul in fascination in the rear view mirror as they communicated in sign language and became acquainted. I had never met a deaf person before or watched sign language. They stirred the air with quick, flexible, snapping movements of their fingers. Their fists opened and closed in a rapid staccato as they slapped or thumped a wrist or their chests.

After watching them for some time I commented to Kirk that I had never seen two people talk so long and fast without getting hoarse. I had no idea what they were saying or how we would communicate during the critical moments that would inevitably occur on the climb because of the potential hazards and shifting mood of the mountain.

Kirk was born with cataracts and had had surgery to remove them when he was two. A not-uncommon result of this surgery was hemorrhaging of blood vessels in the eyes a couple of years later. This resulted in pressure and severe and sudden glaucoma, followed by detachment of both retinas when he was five. Several painful surgeries over the next few years proved unsuccessful in restoring his sight.

Kirk was now nineteen and a student at Washington State University. He was an outdoor enthusiast, had some hiking experience and liked to ski.

He had been recommended to me by Bud Keith. Bud was President of Healthsports, an organization that sponsored skiing trips for the blind and for people with other disabilities, nationally and internationally.

I described the changing scenery to Kirk and recalled some of the efforts involved in getting the project organized. I was president of The Institute for Outdoor Awareness, a company involved in researching the role of wilderness challenge in therapy, education and management development.

JUNE 21, 1981

Nearly two years earlier I had taken a group from a drug treatment center rock climbing in Maryland to learn and share some concepts of trust and communication. We were having lunch as a group next to a river that cut through a vertical uplift of rock. I noticed two small children eight or nine years of age, accompanied by two adults, working their way down from the parking strip along the highway toward the sound of the river. They hugged trees and rocks and reached for the next large object in their path. It became evident that they were blind. They laughed and screamed with delight at everything they touched and explored with their fingers. They were ecstatic when they found the river. I had never seen two children so excited about nature.

In addition to managing a large research grant for the Institute, I was also a management consultant for several agencies in Washington, D.C. and for the City of Philadelphia. I had spent a number of years teaching in Arizona and at the University of Pennsylvania. I had also worked in the White House on some organizational and program issues associated with drug abuse prevention. I traveled to Washington, D.C. a lot and liked to escape into climbing dreams while riding the train back to Philadelphia. After seeing the two children I often wondered how difficult it would be for a blind person to climb a mountain.

One night on the train I tried to imagine a climb with a team of blind climbers and in the process sketched out the project I would later call Pelion.

When I got home I walked over to Fitz's house and described the concept. Fitz, as a psychiatrist whose specialty was working with the blind suggested we talk with Judy Oehler as a sounding board for such an unheard-of project.

Judy was thirty-four and had been living with Type I, commonly known as juvenile diabetes. She had lost her sight when she was twenty-four because of the disease. In spite of her loss of sight she went on to earn a Master's degree in Education and was finishing her Doctorate in Counseling Psychology.

Judy had written to Fitz about some papers he had published, and in the course of their correspondence Fitz learned that Judy had gone through an Outward Bound program. In fact she'd had to initiate legal proceedings because the program refused to accept her. Since they were recipients of federal funding they were governed by the Americans With Disabilities Act and were forced to acquiesce to Judy's request to participate.

When Fitz and I called, Judy at first hesitated, then rejected the concept thinking it an impossibility. After sleeping on the idea overnight she called back and thought it would be a wonderful adventure. Judy subsequently became a tireless and resourceful advocate for the project. When we set out to find funds, equipment and participants, she threw herself into the project with the same determination that she had summoned to work her way through graduate school.

JUNE 21, 1981

An expedition of disabled climbers was unheard of. Most people we had approached for support thought we were crazy and wondered why a blind person would want to climb a mountain. Our insurance broker indicated that not even Lloyds of London would cover us. There was no actuarial base for a team of blind climbers.

Nevertheless, during the first year we identified a small team of blind climbers. Fitz and I described the climb on a radio program broadcast from The Associated Services for the Blind in Philadelphia. Fred Noesner was dialing the Institute before Fitz and I finished the program. His resolute words on the answering machine were, "I am blind. I am thirty-four and I have always wanted to climb a mountain."

Fred lived in a Philadelphia suburb so it was easy to arrange a meeting and go on a simple rock climb in a local park. I was curious as to how this was going to work out. I had never worked with a blind person in a climbing setting.

I picked Fred up at his house and we drove to Fairmont Park. We hiked to a rock outcrop with cliffs of varying degrees of technical challenge. I anchored a loop of rope to a tree at the top of the cliff, snapping a carabiner onto the loop and passed a climbing rope through the carabiner to use this to belay Fred.

In simple terms the carabiner was a pulley at the top of the steep rock outcrop. Fred and I were at the bottom of the outcrop on a park trail. I showed him how to tie into a rope and reviewed the basic commands used by climbers and their belayer.

To belay is to secure the rope so that a climber cannot free fall. We discussed how to maintain three points of contact with rock, either both feet on the rock and one hand, or both hands and one foot, and how to stand to maximize friction. Many beginners become nervous and lean into the rock they are climbing. This pushes their feet away from the rock, making them unstable.

Fred scrambled up the rock as if he had been climbing all his life. As he climbed up, I pulled down the rope passing through the carabineer in order to minimize the slack. If Fred slipped he would not fall. Some joggers going by on the trail watched him for a while, oblivious to the fact that he was blind.

I felt a sense of relief in the realization that the only thing Fred could not do was see what he was doing. Blinded since the age of four by cancer and surgery, Fred now trained other blind people how to use an ingenious optical and mechanical device called an Optacon in order to read regular printed materials. Fred suggested that Doug Wakefield, who had been his first Optacon student, might be interested in the climb.

Doug lived in Arlington, Virginia and worked for the Department of Agriculture in Washington, D.C. as a radio announcer. Anybody living in the Midwest and listening to hog prices had heard Doug. Every morning Doug listened to a number of market recordings, transcribed

JUNE 21, 1981

them into Braille, and at the appointed hour started the farm price broadcast report flawlessly. Doug and his twin brother Dana, a judge in Denver had been born blind.

Fitz was working on a personnel committee for the Associated Services for the Blind in Philadelphia. He happened upon a resume' from Justin McDevitt who was looking for a job. Fitz suggested that I contact him.

Justin McDevitt and his twin brother were born prematurely and medically blinded at birth by excessive oxygen in the incubator. Justin had been working as a social worker in an agency in Virginia that had lost its funding. He was then looking for a job and living with his parents in Villanova, a Philadelphia suburb.

I called Justin and described the project. He was hesitant, concerned about possible dangers and the time it would take that might interfere with his job search activity. I inferred he would become famous and receive job offers. He quickly agreed to participate.

Early in 1980 we had a small team of four blind climbers. We went rock climbing at Carter Rock on the banks of the Potomac River in Virginia and at Ralph Stover Park north of Philadelphia. I soon realized that their not being able to see the mountain or the crevasses and ice-falls above them was not going to be a major factor from a technical aspect. Whether or not the National Park Service would be receptive would be another issue.

PELION

I flew to Seattle to do a little climbing and to visit the Regional Administrator for the National Park Service in Seattle. As I started into the Federal Building on First Avenue to meet the Regional Administrator I wondered what I would do if he didn't think it was safe and would reject the idea.

On impulse I returned to the street to a pay phone and called Jim Whittaker. I had known Jim since 1952. He was instrumental in my getting my first guiding jobs and working for a mining company in Alaska as a technical climber.

Jim Whittaker was a legend in mountaineering. In May of 1963 he was the first American to climb Mt. Everest. When I first met him he managed a small climbing equipment cooperative. The Co-op had started off a few years before as a closet filled with army surplus climbing equipment and some imports in an accountant's office across the hall from the Seattle Mountaineers. Jim took it from an $80,000 a-year business to an internationally known multi-million-dollar-a-year operation called the Recreational Equipment Cooperative, REI.

The "Co-op," for me, was a place to hang out to look at the new equipment and to hear where people were climbing. One day Jim said that a German doctor and his stepson needed a guide and would I take them up Mt. Baker. I was seventeen. It was an amazing request and an amazing experience. I was scared from the beginning to the end.

The next year Jim had referred me to a person who was organizing a climbing team for an exploration mining company in the Fairweather

JUNE 21, 1981

Range in southeast Alaska. I would end up spending two summers with the company, with university in between. Alaska is big and any adventure there was big. My introduction to Alaska was a pivotal point in my life.

My first plane flight took me to Juneau. There I was to rendezvous with a bush pilot named Ken Logan and fly to Lituya Bay the next morning to start setting up camp at the mouth of Coal Creek near the head end of the bay. In the morning I called Ken to schedule the flight. He said he had to fix the wheel that had fallen off his child's tricycle and that we would go out at one o'clock. At one o'clock he said his wife needed the car to go shopping so we would go out at four o'clock. At four o'clock he said the washing machine had broken and he would have to fix it. He thought there would not be enough light to fly up, drop me off and return. We would go out first thing in the morning.

At seven fifteen that night the ground shook under an exceptionally intense earthquake, 8.3 on the Richter scale. A huge landslide at the head end of Lituya Bay generated the largest wave in geologic history. A wall of water 1,800 feet high washed away the side of a mountain, a large forest and what would have been our camp. For the want of a simple tricycle wheel I had escaped doom.

When I called Jim from outside the Park Service lobby in Seattle, he was at home. I asked him if he had ever thought about taking a team of blind people up Mt. Rainier and did he think it was possible. He indicated that he had never taken blind people up but had led a lot of snow-blind people down. Very quickly I described Pelion and he indicated he might be interested in participating.

The Regional Administrator for the Park Service was cordial but eventually got to the question of feasibility. I mentioned that Jim Whittaker thought it feasible and would help out. His response was, "Oh, well, if Jim Whittaker thinks it is okay, we won't argue with him." But he cautioned me that it was not his decision to make and that it would rest with the Park Administrator.

A friend and nurse, Gayle Eversole and I later drove to the park headquarters where I had the same discussion with the Park Administrator. He echoed the sentiments of the Regional official, "If Jim thinks it can be done it is okay by me."

Gayle was a nurse from Philadelphia who had participated in some Institute activities in Pennsylvania and now worked on an Indian Reservation south of Seattle. Two years before she had introduced me to a tribal elder and medicine man, Joe Washington of the Lummi tribe from north of Seattle. I am part Native American and had been trying to organize an outdoor challenge program for Indian youth. Joe Washington was highly respected as the medicine man's medicine man. As Pelion progressed I was hoping that he might provide us with a Safe Journey Blessing.

JUNE 21, 1981

A few days after meeting with the Park Administrator Gayle and I went climbing in the Snoqualmie Pass area for two days. On the morning of the second day we heard a loud explosion. I thought it was a construction crew blasting in the pass below. Later in the afternoon we hiked out. As we started down the highway we noticed that there were not many cars and that those coming from the east, over the pass, were covered with grey ash. The explosion, we later learned, was Mt. St. Helens erupting.

In late 1980 the climbing season for Rainier had passed. I still didn't have funding and a couple of potential team members had dropped out. In November of 1980, Fitz called me late on a Sunday night around 10:00, saying a colleague of his who lived in Washington, D.C. had called a few minutes before. His friend had just returned on a flight from Europe. During the flight seated next to him was blind lawyer named Harold Krentz. Krentz was going to be leaving his law firm to work for President Reagan and heading up a *Hire The Disabled* program as part of the 1981 International Year of Disabled Persons (IYDP).

Fitz's friend gave Krentz's phone number to him and Fitz passed it on to me. I immediately called Harold Krentz, waking him, and gave a quick overview of what I was trying to do. Krentz, sounding a little taken aback at being awakened by a stranger, indicated that he was moving to the White House the next day. He stated the only time we might possibly meet would be early the next morning in his office. I figured he was politely putting me off.

D.C. is only a couple hours' drive from Philadelphia. I was in Krentz's office when he arrived. I described the project in some detail and gave him a copy of the proposal of the project for a team of blind people to climb Mt. Rainier. He suggested that including people with other disabilities should be considered in keeping with the theme of the International Year of Disabled Persons.

Krentz also emphasized that he did not have funds for such a project. I explained I was only interested in an endorsement. Recognition of the project by the White House would help in seeking private funding. Also, the climb would highlight the capabilities of people with disabilities if they were just given a chance.

He took the proposal and said he would get back to me in a couple of weeks because he was moving his office to the White House that afternoon, then leaving for the west coast the next day to represent the President. I also learned that he was going to be working directly for Elizabeth Dole.

When I returned to Swarthmore I called Bud Krogh, a friend whom I had worked for in the White House during the Nixon Administration several years before. We had been friends when I was in high school. I had taken him on some climbs and backpacking trips to remote mountain lakes. He was aware of the project from its inception and had a copy of the proposal. I explained Harold Krentz's new role in Washington and that Krentz worked for Elizabeth Dole. Bud had hired Elizabeth Dole when Nixon was still President. He sent her a copy of the proposal.

JUNE 21, 1981

Two weeks later when Krentz returned from his trip, he did, in fact, approach Elizabeth Dole with the idea. She explained that she knew all about the climb and thought it was a wonderful idea.

Krentz called me to review our timetable and expressed his anger at my having gone above him. My response was that I had a tight timetable and couldn't wait two or three weeks to find out what his response might be. Furthermore, I technically didn't work for him so I did not go above him. Besides, his boss liked the idea.

Harold Krentz, I found later, was a very interesting person. He wrote his autobiography called *To Race The Wind* describing his experiences as a blind Harvard law student. The Broadway play *Butterflies are Free* by Leonard Gersche was loosely based on Krentz's life. Harold was also a musician and a performer, we learned later.

Harold's idea of including members with other disabilities added a new twist and direction to team selection. To assemble the team I contacted dozens of organizations for the disabled, asking for referrals to individuals who might be interested in participating. The National Epilepsy Foundation recommended Richard Rose. Bud Keith, President of Healthsports, recommended Kirk Adams. Healthsports was a unique organization which sponsored skiing trips for individuals who were blind or had some other disabilities that might normally prevent them from skiing. After talking with Bud it became apparent that he would like to join us.

The Washington State Services for the Deaf recommended Paul Stefurak. They also suggested I contact the Services for the Deaf in New York City who in turn recommended Alec Naiman.

I had contacted the Motorola Company to find out if they could provide radios for communications on the climb. The person I talked to, Dave Weisz, pointed out that this would require a communications tower and a permit from the Federal Communications Commission.

During the conversation Mr. Weisz mentioned that Motorola had developed a technique to assist Sheila Holzworth, a young blind woman who ran high school track meets against sighted opponents. Motorola had placed a small radio receiver in Sheila's head band so her coach could transmit directions to guide her to the left or right, and advise when to slow down or speed up.

Sheila, like Kirk, was nineteen. She had lost her sight at the age of eleven in a freakish accident in which the band on her dental braces retainer broke while she was putting on a nightgown. The sharp tines on the retainer gouged out an eye, and the other one had atrophied sympathetically. She continued undaunted by her loss to compete actively in sports.

Charles "Chuck" O'Brien was a lawyer who worked in the same law firm as Clifford Pearlman, a member of the Board of the Institute For Outdoor Awareness. Chuck had been a member of an elite Army Ranger group in Vietnam. He had lost his left leg below the knee

JUNE 21, 1981

when he stepped on a land mine. When I asked him if he wanted to participate he was skeptical, but reviewed his vacation schedule and agreed to join the team. As far as I could tell, he wasn't convinced I was going to pull this project off and seemed to be going along out of curiosity.

Pelion had become a major undertaking. It was an ambitious and daring mountaineering project and had received considerable press coverage. Even the White House, through the efforts of Harold Krentz, was recognizing Pelion, endorsing it as a premier project for the 1981 International Year of Disabled Persons.

Being thoroughly prepared was absolutely essential -- an obsession of mine. In order to anticipate training needs I had taken most of those who lived on the East Coast rock climbing and caving. In rock climbing activities the blind learned knot tying, belaying and rope management as fast as sighted people.

I was fascinated watching Doug and Fred climb. They would search the wall in front of them with their hands, exploring possible foot and hand holds. Once they started to move up the vertical wall they could put the toe of their boots unerringly on the nubbin of rock they earlier had identified as a foot hold. Sighted people always look to see where they are putting their feet. In caving Fred would develop a map in his mind of every turn and incline, crawling on his stomach or walking in a crouched position. He could retrace his steps and guide us sighted participants out of the cave without lights.

PELION

Obtaining proper equipment was also a concern. Initially I wondered how big my credit card bill was going to grow. Slowly, support developed.

When I first contacted Eddie Bauer, an outdoor equipment company, to determine if they could help they responded in the affirmative. I called the person who had mailed me the support letter to find out how much they were willing to contribute to the project. The person's answer was that Eddie Bauer supported "community projects," typically in the range of $400 to $500." I was thinking we needed equipment: ropes, carabineers, ice axes, crampons, boots, tents, stoves, food, parkas, sleeping bags, packs and other items for a total closer to $15,000 dollars. I thanked him for his consideration and asked if I could send him a list of the equipment we needed.

My first experience with Eddie Bauer had been in 1958 when climbing in Alaska. At that time Eddie Bauer was a small firm that made excellent sleeping bags and parkas. Years later they were bought and sold a couple of times and were now part of the Pillsbury corporate structure.

When Fitz, Judy Oehler and I were working out the Pelion concept, Judy mentioned that when she was a child one of her best friends was a Pillsbury family member. She contacted her friend and received an enthusiastic reception to the concept of the project.

When I sent our equipment needs list I was able to comment that the Chairman of the board of the company that owned Eddie Bauer liked the concept of the climb. When an Eddie Bauer representative

JUNE 21, 1981

called me after receiving my list, the first question was, "Was there anything else you need?"

Judy also had contacts with a senior member of Western Airlines who made arrangements for the airline to fly the team members to Denver and from Denver to Seattle and home. This was later amended to fly team members from Seattle to Washington, D.C., then home.

One day I received a call from Philadelphia Life Insurance and was asked if I could come and describe the project to the President of the Company. Fred Noesner lived in a Philadelphia suburb so I picked him up and we went to the Philadelphia Life Insurance Office. We described the project.

When we finished, the president noted that such a project must encounter some cash requirements. He inquired how much we would need as he took out a checkbook and pen. I had probably blinked once or twice computing and suggested $20,000.00. He wrote the check and a photographer came in to take pictures of Fred and me receiving the check. Had I known this was going to happen I might have asked for more!

It was clearly dawning on me that Pelion was supposed to happen and that I was merely doing the facilitating. Everything that was needed was coming with an ease I didn't think possible.

The weeks before the beginning of Pelion were hectic. I was taking groups out climbing, caving, backpacking and canoeing as part of ongoing Institute activity. I was preparing the Institute staff to take over while I was gone. I had to tend to having T-shirts and hats made, making reservations in Aspen, coordinating plane flights, arranging for shipments of equipment and trying to find interpreters for the deaf to meet us in Aspen. In order to provide communications while on the mountain I had to work with the Federal Communications Commission to obtain a radio license and form a radio station. Each day seemed to provide another challenge to be resolved.

I arrived in Aspen a few days before the rest of the team was to arrive in Denver. I wanted to hike the trails, scout training sites and organize what equipment had arrived.

The gateway to Aspen is Independence Pass which is over 12,000 feet high. From the top the highway switches back and forth across the steep mountain slopes by means of hairpin turns so tight that the larger trucks have to stop half-way through and back up before continuing through the turn.

In places the edges of the highway drop several thousand feet to the valley floor below. When I had first traveled over the pass the week before, it was night. I stopped to stretch my legs and hike uphill for awhile. The slope rising to the south was rounded and free of boulders and other obstacles. There was no moon but the stars were brilliant and provided enough light to hike without a flashlight.

As I warmed up I hiked a little faster and noticed a light on the western horizon, like a small sun setting. All the light of stars seemed

June 21, 1981

to run together and disappear into a pinhole which diminished in size. I had flown to Denver from sea level in Philadelphia and driven to 12,000 feet. I found I was running out of breath. When I stopped walking, the pinhole of light expanded and the dark horizon filled with stars. When I started walking uphill the light on the horizon shrank to a pin hole. I experimented walking faster and slower to influence the phenomenon.

It finally dawned on me that I was experiencing oxygen starvation in the cornea, which is not a good thing. I walked slowly back down to the car. There I threw my sleeping bag on the ground and slept until sunrise.

In the morning I drove down to Aspen, then up to the trailhead leading to Buckskin Pass, and hiked to the pass at 12,300 feet between Maroon Bells and Snowmass mountains. This is where we would practice snow climbing techniques. There was a nice meadow at 11,000 feet, surrounded by pine trees and separated from the trail by a stream where we would camp for two nights. Camping and climbing at higher elevations for several days was important for the team members to start their bodies acclimatizing to altitude.

Having organized my thoughts about Aspen and what we would do there, I drove back to Denver to meet the team members who were flying in from around the country.

While going over the pass with Kirk, Alec and Paul, we picked up a hiker going to Aspen. He was carrying a British flag and was from New

Zealand. Paul's eyes lit up and he grinned as he gestured and talked in the muted and unfamiliar verbalizations of a person who had never heard a spoken word. He was excited to communicate that his wife was from New Zealand. We dropped the hiker off at the edge of town and went on to our base of operations, the St. Moritz Lodge.

Fitz and those in Big Blue had arrived several hours before. They had gone hiking and found a restaurant where we could meet. After their hike they returned to the St. Moritz, then went back to the restaurant. Judy and Richard Rose stayed at the lodge to wait for us to arrive.

When we arrived Richard took Kirk, Paul, and Alec to the restaurant. Judy was taking a nap. I had to track down shipments. Some boxes had arrived and more were to arrive the next day. I had to find out where the airport was.

Fitz called the lodge and told me that they were only three blocks away. I called Judy's room and suggested we go meet the rest of the crew. I felt a sense of relief. I felt great. Two years of planning an unprecedented project had come together, and we had a team ready to start training. We would be here for a week, then fly to Seattle and drive to Mt. Rainier.

I waited in the lobby of the St. Moritz for Judy, so we could walk over to join the others. I barely overheard some other guests in the lodge commenting that they had just heard on the evening news that eleven people had been killed on Mt. Rainier earlier in the day.

JUNE 21, 1981

Rainier! Eleven dead! A cold, numbing jolt pounded through me. My legs grew heavy. I was stunned to a standstill. I asked them what else they'd heard. They had no more details. For them it was just a passing news item.

"What had happened? Nothing like this had ever happened before. How would it affect us? Will the team want to continue? Is the mountain safe? Will we be allowed to continue the climb? Will tour sponsors back out? Was it an avalanche? Were the victims experienced?"

Judy arrived and we walked to the restaurant. I did not mention to her what I had just heard. I walked on only vaguely aware of the chilly night air. My mind was echoing questions with no answers. I tried to convince myself that I did not know enough to start worrying.

The team was in an upbeat mood at the La Concina restaurant. They were obviously excited about getting started and hungry from their traveling and hiking. I quietly asked Fitz if he had seen the evening news. None of them had heard about the accident. I told Fitz what I had heard and what I didn't know, then we both circulated around the table informing the others.

Dianne Roberts, Jim Whittaker's wife, and Rick Ridgeway arrived having just flown into Aspen from Seattle. Rick was a world famous mountain climber. He was the first American to climb K2 and the highest peaks on each of the seven continents. He had heard about our adventure from Jim Whittaker and wanted to be our film director. His film crew arrived at the restaurant shortly after Rick.

PELION

Dianne and Jim Whittaker were on the way to the airport when they heard on the car radio about the accident on Mt. Rainier. Jim dropped Dianne off at the airport and drove to Mt. Rainier. She knew that Jim's nephew had been guiding a large party up the Ingraham Ingraham Glacier, the same route that Pelion was to take. The group had stopped to rest and Jim's nephew had moved ahead to set anchors in the steep face below Disappointment cleaver. An ice avalanche crashed down onto the group burying half of them. Jim's nephew was not caught in the avalanche and was able to notify the rangers of the accident.

Jim was to be our climb leader on Rainier. He had stayed in Seattle to scout the route for Pelion and had not planned to meet us in Aspen. Jim is one of the most experienced and strongest mountain climbers in the world. Over the past forty years he and his twin brother Lou, who operated the Rainier Guide Service, had become as familiar with Rainier as anyone could be. Jim and Lou were the ones the National Park Service asked to find out what had happened and to determine if the mountain was safe to climb.

A major storm was now ravaging the slopes of Rainier and it would be several days before Jim would be able to assess the full impact of the accident.

As the word was passed around the table about the accident, I shared that we would have to wait until we heard from Jim and knew more before we could speculate on what it meant for Pelion. Since departing Seattle Dianne had not be able to contact Jim about any details.

JUNE 21, 1981

The feelings at dinner were mixed. Notes were written for the deaf. The blind were asking exactly what an avalanche was. While the news of the accident concerned the group, most of the team was still excited about being in Aspen and getting started. The full impact of the accident didn't set in, at least not overtly.

Several commented that they were going to climb the mountain no matter what. They sounded like the climbers at the turn of the century who would write their wills on the cuff of their shirts before starting a climb. However, during dinner several small group conversations intimated that the news was a little frightening. They were starting to wonder what was really involved in mountain climbing.

After dinner we had a group meeting at the lodge to discuss how we felt. The magnitude of our objective and the tragic loss of eleven lives on our planned route reinforced the need for intensive preparation.

Mt. Rainier rises 14,410 feet above the surrounding countryside. It has the most extensive glacial system in the continental United States. It requires a vertical climb of over 9,000 feet into air that has only half the oxygen as air at sea level. Climbers have to cross narrow snow bridges over crevasses hundreds of feet deep, pass under weathered, crumbling basalt cliffs and avalanching ice falls. The climb would demand that the Pelion members push themselves physically beyond anything they had ever dared before.

CHAPTER 2

JUNE 22: TRAINING, DAY 1

The objectives for the first day were to start pulling the equipment together and to introduce the team to the absolute basics in mountaineering. They were to learn the knots needed to tie into a rope, a mountaineer's way of walking uphill called the rest step, belaying or how to protect one another from a fall, and how to travel as a team with the same pace and rhythm. They would have a strenuous workout.

At the airport Fitz and Justin picked up fifteen large boxes of equipment contributed by Eddie Bauer: packs, parkas, sleeping bags, crampons, stoves, ropes, tents, dehydrated meals and an assortment of other items of climbing gear. These were unboxed and scattered around the swimming pool and courtyard of the St. Moritz Lodge. It was like a giant Christmas party. Equipment was given to each person to sort out and repack into individual units.

General confusion reigned for three to four hours while the many items were sorted out and described to the blind members. Crampons, a frame of metal spikes used to walk on ice, were assembled and fitted to the boots, packs were adjusted and some ill-fitting items were exchanged between individuals.

By three-thirty the equipment was organized enough to allow us to venture out to start training in basic techniques. We took a short drive to a nearby ski slope already cleared of the winter snow by the rains and sun of spring. We put on light packs and hiked up the dirt and rock slope covered with clumps of tall grass and bright red indian paintbrush and other alpine flowers. A few weeks earlier people had been skiing down these very slopes.

The slope steepened and several of the blind people lost their balance and stumbled down slope for a step or two. When this happened, Fitz, Chuck, Richard or I would show them the rest step in which balance is maintained by putting all of one's weight on the downhill foot and relaxing the uphill foot.

The blind could not see the demonstration so they would feel the leg of a sighted person making the step. "Take a breath, relax. Shift your weight up over the uphill foot. Push up. Move the downhill foot up and forward and kick it into the slope. Lock the knee of the downhill leg and settle all your weight onto it. This puts joints over joints and minimizes pressure on the muscles."

"Relax the uphill leg. Let it go limp." These instructions would be repeated over and over for the next two to three days until the motion became automatic. Kicking the uphill foot into the dirt, and later into

JUNE 22: TRAINING, DAY 1

snow, establishes a secure platform on which to stand. This reduces the chances of the foot sliding when weight is transferred to it.

After twenty minutes of hiking up the irregular slope we reached a wide trail cutting across the hill which provided a convenient place to sit and talk. The sun was high in the clear blue Colorado sky and the late afternoon was getting hot. We dropped our packs in a small grove of quaking aspen to take a short rest and breathe in the thin air. This was the first time since arriving in Colorado that we were all in one place without major distractions. I could answer questions about the accident, our schedule and what we had to accomplish over the next few days.

Would we climb Rainier? We still did not know exactly how the climbers had been killed; or the condition of the route; or if the National Park Service would permit Pelion to continue. I took the position that the team would continue to train for the climb. A decision to change the program would not have to be made for five days when we flew from Denver to Seattle. I hoped that by then the weather would have cleared and Jim would have had a chance to scout the route. In case it was not safe, we might consider another route on Rainier.

It might even be necessary to change mountains! Mt. Olympus, on the Olympic Peninsula west of Seattle toward the coast was not as high, but it was a scenic and enjoyable climb. For us Pelion represented an upward step for the disabled. The symbolism of Project Pelion on Mt. Olympus would be poetic.

PELION

Rick Ridgeway had a copy of the morning newspaper which carried the Rainier story on the front page. The tragedy highlighted the seriousness of our undertaking and the need for thorough preparation. For the first time some of the members started to understand the magnitude of what we were going to try to do.

As I was describing the dangers, I remembered being in Jim and Dianne's house a few weeks before and Jim mentioning that a woman had recently been killed rock climbing. Her name was the same as that of a close friend that I hadn't seen for several years. Rick Ridgeway was filming my talk to the group. I started to realize that as I was thinking about the woman and talking to the group, I was crying. It was a strange feeling.

Training continued with belaying practice. Each person was shown how to wrap the rope around his or her waist to get the friction necessary to slow and stop a fall for the person they are protecting. A climbing rope will tear the skin off a person's hands if they try to stop a fall by holding the rope.

The belayer who is higher on the slope sits and braces his or her feet that are spread to form a tripod and faces the climber. The rope is supposed to come between the feet and around the waist. The belayer uses the hand on the rope going to the climber to sense the movement of the climber just as a fisherman would "feel" a line to sense a fish nibbling on bait. The other hand is the "brake" hand and is used to wrap the rope around the waist.

The more contact the rope makes going around the body the greater the friction and stopping power. As a climber ascends the hill toward

JUNE 22: TRAINING, DAY 1

the belayer, the belayer pulls in the rope with the "feeling" hand and pulls it around the waist with the "brake" hand. The trick in belaying is the coordination needed to pull the rope in and never let go of the rope held by the "brake" hand.

Each person was guided through the belaying technique. Then, working in pairs, they tied themselves onto a rope to practice climbing and falling. The ropes used were 160-foot perlon ropes which have a breaking strength of over 5,000 pounds, more than enough to stop a fall as long as the belayer is secure and will not be pulled loose.

Each belayer sat on the ground in such a way as to brace his or her feet and get into a secure position. The person who would be the practicing climber walked thirty to forty feet down the hill and then prepared to climb up the slope as if climbing a cliff. The belayer got into the belaying stance with the rope around the waist and the simulated climb began.

A sequence of verbal signals was used to test the belayer and to indicate when the climber was ready. Verbal signals were not useful with Alec Naiman and Paul Stefurak, the deaf members, so a pattern of tugs on the rope was devised.

First the belayer calls out, "Belay on!"

Next, the climber calls out, "Test One," and pulls on the rope hard enough to straighten it to determine if it is free of obstructions. It is not unusual to pull on the rope only to have it dislodge a loose rock.

Once it is determined that the rope is clear the climber calls out, "Test Two." The climber then pulls hard enough to determine if the belayer is secure and will not be pulled off the cliff or down the slope.

Finally, the climber calls out "Test Three," to determine if the belayer can, in fact, hold the climber in the event of a fall. For this part of the test a couple of people would pull on the rope in sort of a tug-of-war against the belayer.

It is important that the climber knows that the belayer can hold the rope. It is equally important for the belayer to know that he or she can hold the rope. Many people experience a strong sense of responsibility when belaying, knowing that the other person's life might well depend upon their being able to hold the rope.

Once the climber had tested the belay he or she would yell out, "Climbing!" to indicate they were starting the ascent. As the climber started up the slope trying to remember the rest step the belayer practiced the coordinated hand movements necessary to take in the slack in the rope without pulling the climber off balance and not letting go of the rope in the brake hand. The sleight of hand trick that takes most people a few minutes to master is how to place the loose end of the rope from the "brake" hand into the "feeling" hand which holds the loose end while the "brake" hand slides down the rope to the hip area.

Once the "brake" hand has been moved it can pull more rope from around the waist. At the same time the loose end is released by the

JUNE 22: TRAINING, DAY 1

"feeling" hand which reaches down the rope toward the climber and pulls in more slack. If the technique is not done correctly the belayer ends up with a pile of loose rope that will immediately play out if there is a fall. The belayer has to hold the rope around the waist taut at all times.

After a couple of hours of practice, the pattern of setting up a belay stance and testing before climbing became an automatic activity. Each person practiced several rounds of belaying and stopping mock falls. From time to time each climber was instructed to yell, "Falling!" and try to run down the slope and catch the belayer off guard.

Doug Wakefield and some of the other blind climbers tried jumping off the slope, lost their balance and fell over but found they could not move down the slope. With each arrested fall a sense of support, strength and confidence developed. Climbers tried to catch their belayer off guard and always found they were secure.

The slope faced west and the afternoon sun was dropping low when we finished the belay practice. To complete the afternoon training schedule, we formed teams of three climbers on a rope. We planned a climb up the ski slope to practice roped team travel.

The steepness of the slope, the altitude, the rough terrain, different lengths of step and levels of strength, and lateness of the day combined to demonstrate the problems of walking as a unit. In the first few hundred feet some people were pulled up the slope, some down and some completely off balance. Slowly the concept of breathing deeply with each step, the rhythm of the rest step and a coordinated, synchronized pattern of walking evolved as the group climbed three hundred to four hundred vertical feet up the ski slope.

The film crews were seasoned climbers and could anticipate where a team was moving. They would run ahead, set up their cameras and film the climbers as they approached. We had an understanding that they were documenting our effort and not staging a filming expedition.

It had been a long day and Judy was visibly straining to keep up with Rich Rose and Bud Keith. The teams slowly spread apart. Kirk Adams with his youthful energy reserve moved up the slope like he was walking in a park.

At a designated rendezvous point on the slope, we gathered together and sat to relax a while before heading down. The low angle of the sun highlighted the red Indian paintbrush and white crowns of dandelions that were already going to seed. Then, tired from five hours of belaying and hiking above 8,000 feet; and dirty from sitting on the dusty slopes, and thirsty from the exertion in the dry air: we headed down the slope toward the cars and the St Moritz Lodge for a sauna, swim and dinner. It was past ten o'clock when we returned to town. There was a general sense of accomplishment even though some weaknesses and problems were evident.

Fred Noesner, Sheila Holzworth, Doug Wakefield, Bud Keith, Richard Rose and I went to the Aspen city park to cook dinner. We

JUNE 22: TRAINING, DAY 1

wanted to try out the white gas stoves and to sample a dehydrated dinner of beef stroganoff. The others defected to the convenience of a restaurant.

Dinner in the park started quietly. We found a picnic table and bench and spread out the unopened boxes of stoves, cook kits, and food. Fred, Sheila, Doug and Bud studied the equipment as Rich and I unpacked it. Rich had done some hiking and camping and was familiar with the equipment. He set to filling stoves with fuel and to filling the smaller gas bottles from the one-gallon fuel cans while Sheila and Bud sat on the bench and started to make a salad. Suddenly a water sprinkler in the lawn went on, spraying the table and Bud and Sheila. The rest of us escaped the first direct blast of water.

Bud grabbed the pot he was putting salad into and headed in the direction of the water sprinkler. He tried to put the pot over the sprinkler head and got wetter in the process. If he could have seen it he would have walked around behind the sprinkler. A few moments later more sprinklers went on.

Doug went to search for a way to stop the sprinklers. I headed him toward a small building in the middle of the park which might have a shutoff. He moved toward the building at a fast pace without a cane. He stumbled over a couple lying in the grass oblivious to the noise we were making. The couple told him that the sprinkler was on a timer and there was nothing we could do about it. They retreated to the safety of their car.

Rich and I moved the table out of the range of the sprinkler. The meal was continued to near completion before five or six more sprinklers went on, completely covering the area and forcing a rapid evacuation. Everyone grabbed some equipment and started to run to Big Blue in different directions. Rich and I yelled out which way to go. A couple of the sprinklers were the type that shot a pulsing stream of water which first slowly moved across an arc of ninety degrees, then rapidly returned to the original position. The water jet from the sprinkler washed across our table.

Fred thought he would go to the sprinkler and move the head so the water would go in a different direction. When he started out he was moving in the same direction as the advance of the jet of water along its arc so as he moved left the water jet moved left. Fred figured out that the water jet was following him and decided to change his direction to the right. As a matter of coincidence, when Fred changed his direction the sprinkler completed its arc, changed direction and tracked Fred. Fred stopped and yelled, "What the hell! Who is out there?" figuring one of us was tampering with the sprinkler and spraying him.

Bud started muttering about moving faster because we were getting wet and he was getting cold. I started laughing so hard I fell down in near convulsions, started to have an asthma attack and got soaked. My attention turned rapidly from being wet to getting to my pack in the truck where I had my medicated atomizer so I could breathe.

JUNE 22: TRAINING, DAY 1

Fred asked if being asthmatic influenced my climbing. I told him that as a child asthma limited my sports activities so I spent more time with studies. My interests were books and a chemistry set and model building. In scouts our scout leader took four of us up Mt. Olympus on the Olympic peninsula in Washington. I found that above timberline I could breathe and exert myself like I never could at home. Once I found a way into the mountains I found the Seattle Mountaineers, and my life after that was climbing and studying. I climbed and/or skied most weekends for several years, taught climbing, and was active in mountain rescue activities.

We regrouped, agreed on a story of how good our meal was, and made our way back to the lodge where the others were talking about the great meal they'd had at the restaurant. They wondered why we were so wet.

CHAPTER 3

JUNE 23: TRAINING, DAY 2

The morning started before sunrise. I opened boxes, set out piles of food, tents and other items to be divided between the teams. After breakfast everybody started stuffing clothing, equipment and food into their ever-growing backpacks. They groaned with the increasing weight. By noon we were ready to start a three-day outing to get in condition to carry heavy loads for long periods of time.

We drove to the beginning of the Snowmass-Maroon Bells Trail. It looked as if we would run into the sheer face of the pyramid-shaped Maroon Bells peaks if we drove any further. Two-thousand-foot ridges rose steeply above the three miles of valley floor we would hike. The tops of the ridges, barren of trees, were lined with spires, cliffs and huge blocks of rock. Gulleys coming down from the top were filled with giant boulders and debris that had been carried along in the snow avalanches that cascaded down the steep slopes during the winter. Dirt-streaked snow still lingered in the shaded sections of the gullies, and at the higher elevations broad, fan-shaped snow fields expanded out from the base of the cliffs.

PELION

We parked and unloaded the truck and car. Before starting up the trail we sat on the edge of the parking lot in the shade of a small aspen grove and ate a quick lunch of Triscuits, cheese and sausage. A large, flower-filled alpine meadow stretched down to a small lake and across to a dense forest. Birds, flies, and butterflies could be seen reflecting the sun in the distance.

With yells and groans and uncertain expectations everybody hefted their forty-plus-pound packs and started single file across the meadow to the woods of the Snowmass-Maroon Bells Trail. The trail was a three-foot-wide dirt path that wound through waist-high grass and flowers. By the time we crossed the relatively flat meadow the pack straps were already starting to push heavily onto the shoulder muscles.

At the end of the meadow the trail turned right and started up at a noticeable angle. It turned from a dirt trail to an obstacle course through the jumbled pile of the large boulders of the talus slopes that lined the base of cliffs. The trail narrowed and was covered with crushed rock the size of golf balls and tennis balls, and boulders. Large rocks sometimes blocked a part of the trail or forced a small detour.

The blind climbers found different ways to move over the rocky trail. Some walked behind a sighted person, touching or hanging onto a pack or a strap. Fred felt comfortable just walking behind a sighted person listening to the sound of feet on rocks.

Over the past year I had taken Fred on several climbing and caving trips. I found that he could sense trees or follow a trail through

JUNE 23: TRAINING, DAY 2

the bushes and flowers by listening to the echoes bouncing off leaves. While he walked he generated sound waves by slapping his pants legs, or drumming his fingers on his hard hat. In the city he had taps on the heels of his shoes to generate the sounds for echoes.

Others climbers hung onto the pack of the person in front almost to the extent of being pulled up. Travel was slow and unsteady but the team kept moving. An assortment of expressions could be heard as different people stumbled on the larger rocks or when a rock tipped over, pitching a person off balance. A stream fifteen feet wide flowed across the trail. An uneven sequence of rocks rose just above the water and some were washed over by the jumping water.

The stream was noisy and disorienting. Each blind person had to balance on one foot on a rock and search with the other foot for the next rock with a sighted person indicating how much to the left or right or straight ahead the foot had to be moved. I found that tapping on the target rock with my ice axe provided sufficient orientation for several of the blind climbers who had lost their sight before the age of five.

Nobody wanted to miss a rock and fill their boots with water or slip off and fall in. The water was deep enough and swift enough to wash away any loose items that fell in. The crossing was made with teetering balance and small slips but without any drastic events. A demonstration of courage and tenacity was emerging.

Every twenty minutes or so somebody would want to stop and adjust a strap; rebalance their pack; or lean their pack on a rock to get the pressure off their shoulders and feet for a few minutes. I had to play the role of a drill sergeant to keep them going. If the team had to stop every time one member did, we would never get up the trail. We tried to go for forty-five minutes to an hour, then take a break where everybody stopped.

During the short breaks everyone would take a quick sip of water or juice and put on sun cream and insect repellent. It was warm. Sweat evaporated rapidly in the low humidity of the higher altitude.

During one of these breaks Doug sounded like he was muttering to himself about a problem and I went over to find out if he was okay. He affirmed that he was fine and explained that friends of his at National Public Radio had loaned him some lightweight recording equipment. He had taped a microphone to his climbing helmet and was recording his feelings and observations along with the sounds of packs squeaking and his boots scraping rocks. Throughout the trip Doug could be heard talking to himself as he recorded.

Hikers coming down the trail were confronted with a line of thirteen people. Some seemed confused and others stood aside in awe. Some didn't seem to comprehend, some turned away in embarrassment, and some just stood there and stared until the team disappeared from sight.

After two-and-a half hours of nearly non-stop hiking we paused for a long rest. Everybody had a chance to sip some juice, get away

JUNE 23: TRAINING, DAY 2

from the weight of their pack, lie back and listen to the birds and insects.

I reviewed with the team members who were there where we wanted to get to today. The team was spreading out and it would be unreasonable at this stage to hold everybody back waiting for a few slower members. On the return trip and on Rainier the group would travel as one. I described to Chuck the meadow we would camp in. "You will find it after you cross a small stream flowing straight down the valley. It is a large meadow on the south side of the stream. It's the only stream you will cross."

Judy, following Fitz, was lagging behind. I decided to walk with her to help reinforce the rest step and her breathing. It was apparent that she was physically weaker than other members of the team. Fitz started up the trail with Doug.

Judy and I rested for ten minutes before we started out. She hung on to a strap on my pack. "Step, breath, relax. Step, breath, relax. Step, breath, relax." I chanted.

From time to time I broke the monotony of my instruction with a description of the passing scenery.

"We are entering a small pine grove where trees have been knocked down by an avalanche. Can you smell the pitch? For some reason it always reminds me of fresh blackberry pie."

"Step, breath, relax. Step, breath, relax. Step, breath, relax."

"Do you feel that breeze flowing down the gully on our right? It is still filled with snow higher up."

"Step, breath, relax." With every word "step" I planted my foot hard enough so Judy could hear it hit the ground and feel my pack hesitate as I relaxed and took a breath. I exaggerated my breathing so she could hear each inhale and exhale. Actually, the emphasis was not entirely for her benefit as I was still adjusting to the altitude and my hundred-plus-pound pack.

After an hour she was moving smoothly and rhythmically and found a pace which was synchronized with her breathing. Doug and Fitz came into view higher up on the switchbacks of the trail. Twenty minutes later Judy and I slowly caught up and passed them. I felt encouraged by Judy's ability to move. She had looked weak the day before and I was hoping that more expert technique would offset her apparent lack of strength.

We caught up with the rest of the party in a small sloping clearing on the downhill side of the trail. They had stopped and were setting up tents and starting to relax. Paul and Alec already had a stove purring. "Purring" is the best term I know to describe the sound made by a Svea or Primus white gas stove. When one is cold and hungry it is the most welcome sound imaginable. The film crew was busy documenting how blind and deaf climbers were working together to put up a tent.

JUNE 23: TRAINING, DAY 2

Judy and I stopped. I started to take off my pack but thought "NO! This was not our plan. We were three-quarters of a mile short of the meadow. I let everyone know that this was not the spot, that they would have to repack and continue. I reassured Judy I would come back and get her.

There was a general grumbling and it was apparent they were tired and unhappy with my decision. I left and continued up the trail and they followed after repacking. Judy stayed with Fitz and Doug.

I made good time getting up to the meadow and dropped my pack where the center of camp should be and headed back down the trail. I met Kirk, Sheila and Chuck and let them know it was at least twenty minutes up and they should use my pack as a reference point. I passed the other members and found Judy, Fitz and Doug ready to move uphill.

The film crew said they were going to stay because the light would be low and they would not be able to do any more filming. It occurred to me that the making of the early camp might have been suggested by the film crew because of the loss of light. I talked to Rick and suggested that I did not want filming to dictate what we did, where we did it and how we did it.

I took Judy's pack and we headed up the trail. Just before sunset everybody was in the meadow. It was the size of a football field and flat. There was easy, safe access to the stream for water and a view of the Maroon Bells was unobstructed. We were at 11,000 feet and the air was crisp. This was to be home for the next two nights.

PELION

Dianne left her pack and went back down the trail to go to Aspen to try to contact Jim for information about climbing conditions on Rainier.

As we set up tents the tops of the peaks turned brilliant orange then crimson as the sun set, becoming a pale shadow grey against a darkening sky.

Kirk made a fresh salad, chopping and slicing the lettuce, cucumbers, tomatoes, cheese and lunch meat into a large plastic bag. This was also known as garbage bag salad, a useful technique for making salad for group hiking in windy sand dunes. I prepared dehydrated vegetable stew and Fitz started brewing coffee. This was the first time the whole team had eaten together outside. Some had misplaced their spoons or cups or plates.

There were no tables or chairs. Everybody tried to sit as close to the stove and coffee pot as possible. I paced around the cooking area trying to keep the others from stepping onto a cooking pot or from kicking over the stove. Justin turned out to be a menace because he kept moving around. Patterns of personality were starting to emerge.

The salad was great, the stew was great, the coffee was great, but pudding for desert was missing. Meals and food packages had been scattered throughout several packs. A search was made but the pudding could not be found.

Everyone crawled into their tents for the night. Kirk, Justin, and Rich were in the same tent and could be overheard talking about the

JUNE 23: TRAINING, DAY 2

accident on Rainier. Justin's concern was noticeable. "People died; it's kind of spooky. We are going to be there and we don't know how they died."

"Some people are going to wonder what right we have to go up there after others died." Kirk started to dwell on reactions that might influence the climb.

"Hey guys," Rich broke in, "we have to trust our leadership. They are not going to let us get into trouble. What we have to do is go out there and blow everybody's minds."

I decided to sleep out under the stars. It would be nice to be alone for a few minutes to try to sort out the experiences of the past two days. Some of the concerns of all expedition leaders were starting to show up. Personality issues, fears and balance in responsibility. I wanted to turn more responsibility over to others but the uniqueness of the team and time pressures frustrated me. We had a full-fledged mountaineering expedition and none of the people were mountaineers or even familiar with the ethics or leadership concepts of mountaineering.

Over the past seven months I had pulled the team together. My main criteria for accepting them as team members was their willingness to make a commitment to the project, their personalities, and then outdoor experience -- or lack of it. Though I had talked to them on the telephone and corresponded with Alec and Paul, I hadn't met most of them until we arrived in Denver and still didn't know them very well.

PELION

About the time I started to wonder what I had gotten myself into, a shooting star streaked across the sky and disappeared behind the mountain fortress above us. Sheila's voice carried across the meadow, "Goodnight, Uncle Phil."

CHAPTER 4

JUNE 24: TRAINING, DAY 3

Rick Ridgeway woke me up with his huffing and puffing like a small train as he stomped heavy-footed into camp carrying two large, heavy packs. Combined, they were as big as he was. Rick is a world class climber who has managed to get on some of the most spectacular climbs in the world because of his combined climbing and filming skills. He and the rest of the film crew had spent the night in the small clearing half-an-hour below us and were trying to arrive at our camp before everybody was up.

The air was clear and the temperature was thirty-four degrees. I let out a few yodels to stir the others and shook Paul and Alec to get them started. Everyone moved slowly out of their warm sleeping bags and tents into the meadow. Fitz lit the stoves and started a pot of coffee. He prepared a batter of pancake mix and fed people as they emerged from their tents. It seemed easier to stand and eat the pancakes than to sit on the damp ground. Judy took her insulin. Several people expressed pleasure with their first experience of sleeping in a tent in a sleeping bag.

After breakfast the water bottles were filled and stuffed into small day packs along with cheeses and sausage for lunch, light clothing and sun cream. When everyone was ready we started up the Snowmass-Maroon Bells Trail again to go to Buckskin Pass. At the pass there were steep snow slopes where we could practice snow climbing techniques.

The trail climbs a few hundred feet higher before breaking above timberline in a broad, alpine, V-shaped valley where it divides at the junction of two streams. One stream comes down the valley from the north and the other from Buckskin Pass to the west. We followed the trail heading toward Buckskin Pass. It crossed back and forth across the slope of the ridge separating the two streams and eventually crossed to the left directly under the pass.

Hiking through this alpine meadow stimulated every sense. Small flowers grew everywhere and sparkled in the sun. They filled the air with a fragrance that mingled with the odor of perspiration from the effort of travel and the warmth of sun, and the aroma of sun cream. Water cascading over boulders gurgled and splashed a light spray which cooled the skin on bare arms and faces, accentuating the sensory experience of alpine travel.

Aluminum cups dipped in the stream were instantly cold. A drink from an alpine stream where the water has poured over rocks is an intensely refreshing experience. Water from melting snow has no minerals and no taste. Almost as tasteless were the endless jokes and stories Bud Keith told as he hiked.

JUNE 24: TRAINING, DAY 3

After two hours of hiking the team had slowly spread out. Kirk and the younger team members were half an hour ahead of the last team. I had them wait at a small snow slope that blocked the trail before continuing the steep climb up the last eight hundred feet to the pass. My concern was that someone higher on the trail might dislodge rocks onto the party below. It would be safest if we traveled as one group.

While waiting for Judy and Rich I showed Fred, Sheila and Kirk how to glissade, which is like skiing without skis. We climbed up the snow slope for thirty to forty feet and then glissaded down to the others. The slope wasn't steep enough and the snow was too soft to go more than a few feet at a time, but they had their first exposure to sliding down a slope on their feet. They also learned a little about kicking their feet into the snow hard enough to make a good step to stand on. They found that the rest step works nicely on snow. They also found that when snow is a little soft each hard kick sprayed the snow up into their faces and up their pant legs.

The others munched on a mixture of nuts, raisins and M&Ms called Gorp and listened to Bud tell stories. Bud, it seemed, had a story or a joke for every occasion. Few of them could be told in mixed company. There was some concern early on that Bud's stories might not be appropriate for Sheila. It did not take long to find out that Sheila did not need any protecting.

The slope became steeper and the trail cut back and forth across the rock and dirt-filled trough leading to the pass. Doug commented that the switchbacks disoriented him. I gave everyone constant reminders to breathe deeply and to use the rest step.

Buckskin Pass is a saddle at 12,300 feet. Ridges rise above the pass five to eight hundred feet to the north and south and the trail dropped into the valleys on the east and west. We had come up the trail from the east which leads under the north face of Maroon Bells peaks. The trail dropping off the west side goes into a valley below the northeast flank of Snowmass Peak.

A few feet north of our trail was a large snow patch and the melted remnants of a cornice, an overhanging ledge of snow. The top of the snow patch was vertical for eight feet. The angle of snow tapered off and flattened onto a shelf fifteen feet wide before dropping off vertically and merging with the rock and grass-covered slope leading to the valley floor.

The clear blue sky behind the peaks to the east highlighted the broken skyline of craggy summits and ridges. Small shadows from puffy cumulus clouds drifted across the forest below and climbed the barren rock cliffs. To the west the broad summit of Snowmass Mountain blocked the horizon.

The steep snow slope was an ideal setting to review belaying and kicking steps and climbing a snow slope as steep as a ladder. Here the team would also learn how to use an ice axe to make a self-arrest, the technique of stopping oneself when falling down a steep snow slope. Throughout the day each person had a chance to belay another

JUNE 24: TRAINING, DAY 3

person who would practice climbing and falling. When belaying, a person sat on an unused coil of rope, which served as an insulator from the snow. They were also anchored to an ice axe shoved into the snow so they could not be pulled off the top of the slope. They would spread their legs, dig their heels into the snow and wrap the climbing rope around their body just as they did on the ski slopes outside of Aspen.

They wore gloves to prevent rope burn when the smooth rope slid through their grasp as their climber jumped off the edge. As they wrapped the rope further around their body the falling climber was stopped. The climbers were to step backward off the edge of the steep section and then climb back to the top. In turn, each person was tied onto the climbing rope and instructed on how to hold the ice axe to use it for a self-arrest in case they fell on a steep snow slope.

In the self-arrest, the ice ax is held diagonally across the body from one shoulder to the opposite hip. The axe has a pointy pick and a spoon-shaped adze. The pick of the axe is pointed forward and the adze back over the shoulder. The arm holding the head serves as a shock-absorber to keep the ice ax from being wrenched out of the climber's hands if the pick gets stuck in a crack, hard snow or ice.

When sliding down a slope the climber maneuvers to get onto his stomach with the feet downhill, then spreads his legs, digs his toes into the slope and makes an arch by raising his buttocks up. The chest is pushed down on the ice axe and forces the pick into the slope. This results in three points of contact with the slope--the toe of each boot and the pick of the ice axe. I instructed each person, signing and gesturing to the deaf, waiting for acknowledgment of comprehension by either gesture, words spelled out in sign language or lip reading.

Communicating with different team members varied. At times I pulled out a tablet and wrote out my message or asked Paul or Alec to write out their messages. Deaf since early childhood, both of them had speech impediments that further limited our ability to communicate. Communicating or demonstrating with the blind climbers was more tactile. It was necessary to lead them through the motions, pushing or pulling arms, fingers or feet as necessary.

Once they were ready I asked each person to back up until he or she stepped off the vertical edge of snow. The valley behind the climbers gave the illusion of awesome height. I would describe the setting to those who were blind but had the feeling the descriptions were abstract. What they would experience, however, would be real. As they stepped over the edge, sometimes with hesitancy, and always with an exclamation, they went into the self-arrest position.

They stopped their initial fall fifteen to twenty feet down the slope. Then they were instructed to walk another twenty to thirty feet down to the bottom of the slope. I would then glissade down to them. Each was then instructed how to use the ice axe to climb back up the hill. As they started up I climbed up alongside them and reminded them to breathe. "Breathe deep; breathe so the people on top can hear you."

JUNE 24: TRAINING, DAY 3

They climbed straight up the slope and over the vertical section. This slope was steeper than anything anticipated on Rainier. There were no technical difficulties but each person found that the exertion at an altitude of 12,300 feet had a noticeable effect on his or her breathing. It was exhausting.

Charles "Chuck" O'Brien had been an avid outdoor and adventure enthusiast as a teenager. He had joined the army and was a Special Forces instructor and ranger in Vietnam. He lost his left leg just below the knee when he stepped on a land mine. He now wore a leg prosthesis which was held to a short leg stump below the knee. The prosthesis had a slightly hinged ankle which made it possible for Chuck to walk with a gait that was nearly indistinguishable from that of a person with two normal feet.

Once I had Chuck accompany me on a management orientation rock climbing trip with a group from Philadelphia. The people in the party did not know that Chuck was missing a leg. It was interesting to see their reactions at the end of the day when they climbed into the van complaining about how difficult some of the pitches had been. Chuck climbed into the van last, sat on the floor and took off his prosthesis, and sighed and commented how good it felt to take it off.

None of them had seen an artificial leg before. They had not noticed all through the day that he walked or climbed differently than anyone else, only that he climbed better than most in the group. I knew then that Chuck would not have problems on a climb of Rainier. However, walking on a street or rock climbing is different than climbing a near-vertical snow slope.

In order for Charles to climb the steep slope he first anchored the ice axe firmly in front of him. Then he had to reach down and grab the prosthesis near the ankle, maneuver his prosthesis with his hand to get his left foot high enough for a step then slam it into the slope with enough force to knock out a small ledge. Sometimes he had to swing the foot into the slope a couple of times in order to make a ledge big enough for his left boot. Hanging onto the ice axe he could then balance and stand on the toe of his false left foot, then raise and kick his right foot into the snow higher on the slope. Then he would pull the ice axe out of the snow, anchor it as high above him as possible and lift his left leg a little, reach down, grab his left knee, raise it higher, grab his ankle and then thrust his left foot into the slope, and test it with his hand. He would then raise his body up on his false leg and start the cycle over. Through perseverance he worked his way up to and over the vertical section of snow.

As a joke he had put sun cream on his wooden leg to guard it against the intense sun and its reflection off the snow.

This was the team's third day at the higher altitude. When they weren't belaying or climbing, they hiked around with the film crew, rested, nibbled at lunch, swapped stories and napped. Inside they were changing. Their bodies were generating more red blood cells to more effectively capture the oxygen from the thinner air.

JUNE 24: TRAINING, DAY 3

Each time I instructed one of them and followed them down and up the slope I felt a growing sense of strength in the team. Each person was willing to try. Each person grasped the concepts. Even if apprehensive, each stepped off the steep slope. As each person climbed back to the top and said, "Belay off," I could feel an increase in desire to get to the next person to see how he would do. Each person getting to the top was a confirmation that we could do it. We could climb Rainier. But we still didn't know if we would receive permission to try.

Late in the afternoon the procession was getting ready to start down the pass toward camp. I said, "We have to get down before it gets dark."

Sheila, blind of course, responded quickly, "Hey, man; it is dark."

Spirits were high. Judy and I started down last. After a few minutes of descending on the trail, I noticed the film crew frantically gesturing upward. Four mountain goats were grazing along the shoulder of the slope separating the northern valley and the pass. They were fifty feet above us. We stopped and stood motionless as they slowly moved out of sight from right to left, unperturbed by our presence.

I described to Judy how they grazed, nibbling and munching off the tops of bushes and grass. Occasionally one would stop, stare down at us, switch its tail and go on nibbling. It would have been enjoyable to spend more time watching but we had to get to camp.

The team continued down the trail, a blind person touching the pack of a person in front. Each sighted person developed a different method of calling out rocks and obstacles. Some terms had become codes. "Barrier," for example, meant that a small diagonal curb had been made of rocks to direct water off the trail. It was usually a matter of stepping over the barrier. When there were too many rocks to describe a simple step or two, it would be necessary to slow down to give the follower time to pick a way through.

I found myself consumed with an awareness of every loose rock and obstacle and tried to shape an image of the trail with words. I banged my ice axe against rocks to create a sound to mark their location and moved my pack to indicate where the blind person following should step.

Much of the guiding was done by movement of the pack. If it went up and down, that usually meant a big step. If the motion of the pack went straight ahead, but was rotated sideways, the signal was to walk around in the direction of the pack rotation. In effect, a plumb line dropped from the center of the back of the pack would have scribed out a line on the trail. Whenever the going was easy the pace increased, and when there was uncertainty, the pace would be slowed. Most of the blind climbers following directly behind the guide could detect the obstacles by sounds. We reached the meadow a little after 7:30. The white gas stoves were lit and water pots put on for coffee and dinner.

I looked up from the cooking pot of dehydrated chicken and rice to see Kirk running alone down the hill from a grove of small pine trees

JUNE 24: TRAINING, DAY 3

where he had gone to relieve himself. Some of the climbers just lay back and relaxed. Chuck's knee stump was already starting to blister and he needed to bathe it. Fred, guided by the sounds of the stream, the meadow and the stoves helped by going over to the stream for fresh water and then to the stoves to heat the water for Chuck. From time to time Chuck could be heard to say "Over here Fred." Anybody walking by the camp would not be able to tell by the level of activity that anyone was blind.

While dinner was cooking somebody suggested that tuna would be good in the salad. Doug said he had tuna fish-- twelve small cans in his pack-- and mouths started to water. Then Doug pulled out the missing cans of pudding. A few minutes later Justin stepped on the box of eggs that he had carried up from the cars the day before. While looking for the tuna fish he had taken the eggs out of his pack, set them on the ground and forgotten them.

Justin McDevitt had been blind since birth. Though originally apprehensive about coming on the trip, he wanted to experience more of the world and to do something challenging. He was raised in a family that traveled, he was fairly cosmopolitan, well read and somewhat like an absent-minded professor, setting things down and forgetting them.

Justin was constantly on the move and bumping into or stepping on something. I couldn't get him to sit still and was constantly on guard that he would step on the stove or knock a meal over. Trying to get him to stay in one place was impossible. I was already starting to wonder what he would walk on when we were on a glacier and he was wearing crampon spikes on his boots.

PELION

The evening was cool and the clouds that had formed during the day looked as if they would dissipate. Fitz, Kirk and Sheila also decided to sleep in the open. A few shooting stars and a satellite ended the day.

How do you describe a star to a blind person?

CHAPTER 5

JUNE 25: TRAINING, DAY 4

The moon rose about two o'clock into a clear sky. Even though it was only a partial moon, it was so bright it woke Fitz up. He watched a shooting star and went back to sleep. The morning sky was bright by 5:30. I put the coffee pot on the stove at 6:00 and started shaking tents. A long day was planned and I wanted to get packed and on the trail as soon as possible. The objectives for the day were to hike out to the cars, drive to Aspen, buy food, put in an afternoon of rock climbing, and then drive to Independence Pass.

The broken eggs were used to make French toast a la Justin. While we packed and ate, Fitz as team physician (or doc) made rounds tending to sore muscles, headaches from the altitude, infected throats, diarrhea and blisters. As a psychiatrist he diagnosed that some of the complications were nervous reactions.

The trail switched back and forth down the shoulder of a ridge for two miles and emerged above Crater Lake. Travel down the steep trail seemed easy and there was little stumbling and tripping. An efficient working relationship was developing between the sighted and the blind. Describing the obstacles was less of a conscious effort. My mind was filling a little with pride in the team. Could anybody really believe what was happening?

Crater Lake is a popular day trip for hikers, and the closer the team got to the end of the trail the more hikers we encountered. Some carried picnic baskets, some had noisy radios. There were a number of young couples strolling up the trail hand-in-hand; there were parents with children on their backs.

The reactions of the hikers were mixed as they met the Pelion team coming down the narrow rock-and-boulder-strewn trail. At first some stared defiantly as they hiked closer, as if to say, "I'll take the middle of the trail...you step aside." As the distance shortened, their awareness of something unusual set in. When they realized that the second and third person, carrying huge packs, were blind, they stepped aside.

Some looked shocked and just stared, some said hello, and others were more euphoric and shared a sense of joy in the accomplishment they were witnessing. They all just stood and watched each blind climber hike down the trail until he or she disappeared, only to be surprised when they turned to continue up the hill and encountered the next group from Pelion.

What must they have thought when Fred went by? Fred traveled the greater part of the trails unaided. Usually he followed a few steps behind someone else and sensed the terrain by the sounds and echoes of boots on rocks. He has a method of walking that works well on trails. He stands

JUNE 25: TRAINING, DAY 4

erect and his center of gravity seems low. He moves forward from the hips so he isn't thrown off balance when his foot hits a rock or log. He only moves forward when his leading foot is secure.

Somebody called Fred's gait the "blind man shuffle." Judy said that when she went blind she was taught not to use the "shuffle" because it would identify her as blind. Judy's method of walking was different from Fred's. She walked more like most sighted people, leading from the shoulders with her center of gravity of the body above the hips. This is an unstable posture when walking over rough and uncertain terrain.

A large number of people encountered on the trail seemed embarrassed or frightened. It looked as if they were afraid they might catch something. Others looked confused as if they were supposed to do something, or help, and didn't know how. Some seemed to find a knot of compassion and emotion inside and didn't know what to do with their feelings. Some cried.

From time to time Judy would ask Rich, "How much further?...Do we have far to go?... When can we stop?"

These questions, asked by everybody, often reflecting fatigue, were handled by different members in different ways.

"Just a little further."
"We'll be there when we're there."
"I think it's just around the corner."
"I see the lake, it can't be too far."

Rich kept telling Judy, "Four hundred yards;" and a little later, "Four hundred yards."

The answer was always, "Four hundred yards."

The question of how the blind deal with a sense of distance in order to budget their remaining energy is an interesting and important one especially in climbing. A sighted climber can look up a slope and judge its steepness, slow down and go into low gear physically. A blind climber has to be in good condition and has to budget their energy output. Their guide has to be sensitive to their strength and be able to judge the effect of the pace on energy requirements.

At trail's end the camera crew staged a couple of scenes with the first team down. A local television station and reporters filmed the climbers coming out of the woods and sauntering the last quarter mile through the meadow above Crater Lake, the imposing peaks of the Maroon Bells in the background. Some climbers arrived at the parking lot and collapsed to the ground in order to slide out from under their packs. Others stood there and smiled a sense of accomplishment as they took a drink of water and were helped out from under their packs.

The packs were lashed, two deep, on top of Big Blue. With yells of bravado and the aroma of sweat and sun cream, we headed for Aspen to pick up some extra supplies and to make some adjustments in schedule. Chuck found that the strain of hiking, climbing and the unusual use of his prosthesis caused severe blistering on his

JUNE 25: TRAINING, DAY 4

stump. He was going to stay at the St. Moritz to rest his leg and call Pennsylvania to see how his wife was doing. She was expecting twins any day.

Rather than have a restful two days while we practiced rock climbing techniques and did higher altitude hiking, Chuck took on the task of getting extra gear shipped to Seattle and renting another car. We had picked up so much equipment we couldn't fit everybody into Big Blue and the car we had already rented.

Dianne Roberts decided it was best for her to leave for Seattle early. She had grown sensitive to the need for a day or two in Seattle. She would be able to check with Jim Whittaker about the weather conditions on Mt. Rainier, do some shopping, pull together some loose ends of equipment and improve on the brand of cheese and salami we had for lunch.

I had only met Dianne briefly before the evening in La Concina. During the past four days her keen sense of observation and insight into the moods and needs of people became more and more apparent. Her skill of observation had been sharpened by expedition climbing experiences with Jim on Everest and K2, the two highest mountains in the world. She provided a sympathetic and understanding ear to those growing weary from their heavy packs and long trails. I wondered from time to time how much chaos there might have been without her laughing smile which touched and helped everybody at one time or another.

PELION

Once, as Alec watched her hike down the trail, he signed a sigh and indicated how lovely he thought she was. I signaled back how big her husband was.

By noon we left Chuck and Dianne and headed out of town to spend the afternoon rock climbing. The director of the Aspen Climbing School volunteered his services. He led us to an area off the highway called "The Grotto" where we could practice rope techniques that would be useful in the event someone fell into a crevasse on Rainier. He hung ropes from the top of a four-hundred-foot cliff. The movie crew wanted to film a member of the Pelion team going up the rope using a mechanical device called a jumar. A jumar slides up the rope but not down. A three-foot-long piece of rope with a loop at one end is attached to the jumar. The climber places one foot in the loop and stands on it. By sliding the jumar up the climbing rope a foot and a half, then standing on the loop, the climber has moved a foot and a half up the cliff. By using two jumars it is possible to develop the equivalent of a portable ladder.

Kirk was given instruction on how to use the technique. He placed a foot in each loop, raised his right foot and the right jumar at the same time, and then stood up on his right foot. Then he raised his left foot and jumar up to the right jumar and stood on his left foot. By repeating the process he proceeded to climb for more than one hundred feet up the rope secured to the top of the cliff.

Kirk had lost his sight when he was six. His father was a high school sports coach and Kirk was raised to be active and independent. He

JUNE 25: TRAINING, DAY 4

enjoyed out-of-door activities and participated in the Ski-For-Light program administered by Bud Keith. Kirk had just finished his freshman year at Washington State College and was on summer leave. He moved around camp, ran down hills and climbed with the ease of a sighted person.

People driving to Independence Pass from Aspen could see Kirk suspended high above the highway on one rope and a camera man and camera hanging from another rope. They no doubt wondered about the daring of people who do such things. Could they have comprehended a blind person's desire to climb? Or even believe the person they saw was blind?

While Kirk was working with the film crew I set up two other ropes on some large boulders for the others to practice the use of prusik (pronounced PROO sick) loops to climb up a rope. The prusik loop is a ten to twelve-foot loop of quarter- inch rope which is tied around the climbing rope with the prusik knot. The prusik knot can be moved up a rope when there is no pressure on the knot, but grips the rope when weight is put on the loop and doesn't slide down. It would be useful in the same way as the Jumars in helping a person climb out of a crevasse. Prusik knots had been used for years before the mechanical devices like the Jumar were developed. It is the same knot that flag pole painters use to get to the top of a flag pole.

To use the prusik knot the loops are passed inside the climbing rope around the climber's waist and the climber stands in the two of them, one for each foot. In an alternating fashion the climber stands on one loop and takes the weight off the other. He then slides the one without the weight on it as far up the climbing rope as possible and then shifts the weight to stand on the loop which has just been raised. The shifting of the weight secures the loop and frees the other prusik knot so it can be raised. The two knots become a sliding ladder which can be used to climb up a cliff or out of a crevasse on a glacier.

Using Prusik knots is simple in principle but requires coordination. Each person took turns standing in the prusik slings, hanging on the climbing rope, and spinning in a circle as they struggled with the knots. They had to climb up fifteen to twenty feet and then come down. In addition to the two loops that a person stands in, a third prusik sling is used around the chest to hold the person upright. With three knots on the climbing rope each climber had to find the knot he was going to move, and then search with their hands as to where the knot would be moved.

The knot on the loop that a person is standing on is jammed tight and cannot be moved which means that only the two knots that do not have pressure on them can be moved. Sometimes when tired a climber will have pressure on all three knots. They cannot move up or down the rope until they release pressure on a loop and un-jam the knot.

Prusik knots are not high technology but there are some considerations. We used quarter-inch manila rope because it would not stretch. If the prusik loop is made of thin cord that stretches it will seize and can only be released by cutting it off.

JUNE 25: TRAINING, DAY 4

When descending with prusik knots the process is reversed. The lowest knot is moved down and the weight then taken off the higher knot so it can be moved down. If on the way down the top knot is moved too far, it will jam on the lower knot, or if the bottom loop was moved too far down and the weight of the body lowered, the top knot would be out of reach.

Fred, Judy, Sheila, Doug, Bud and Justin couldn't see the knots they had tied and manipulating them was like a complex and exhausting puzzle. Adjustment to altitude was not complete, and the exertion of fighting the knots, raising and hanging on by one hand, and balancing while spinning in the air was very tiring. Sometimes they would get stuck and hang there ten to fifteen minutes while they figured out how to un-jam a knot.

Apart from setting up the exercise and demonstrating how to tie and use the knots, and an occasional comment of encouragement, I let each person suffer through the problem. They, after all, had to climb every step on Rainier on their own and each had to be capable of getting out of a crevasse if necessary. Watching them gave me some idea of how they might respond if they got stuck and stressed on the climb.

The afternoon passed. The ropes were taken down and coiled and we started back over the pinecone-covered granite slabs toward the cars to drive toward Independence Pass. In order to get to the cars we had to drop down a steep grade to reach the road. This put us on the blind side of an extremely sharp curve. Cars and motorcycles zipped around the turn without much warning. I wanted to get to the bottom of the grade before Alec or Paul did, anticipating and trying to avoid their taking the blind climbers across the highway. Without their sense of hearing I wasn't sure they could detect a car coming around a turn or in which direction a blind person might move if they were in the middle of the highway when a car approached.

I was delayed helping somebody over a steep section and Alec got to the bottom. He immediately started to lead two of the blind climbers across the road. I shouted down for them to wait until I got down to where they were. They shook off Alec's hand and refused to go with him. By the time I reached them Alec was fuming. He accused me of treating him like a second-class citizen. He had come on the trip to demonstrate what a deaf person could do and I was treating him like the rest of society did, not trusting him.

I could sense his anger, and I also felt bad about the situation. I tried to explain that my first concern was safety and I still didn't know him well enough, or his capabilities or the capabilities of the deaf population in general. Until I did I would not put him and others into what I considered a treacherous situation.

Paul and Alec carried out their anger to a childish and more dangerous level. They would lie down or sit in the middle of the highway and jump up pretending a car was coming, and then dance around like it was a big joke.

Some of the problems of being deaf and working with the deaf were becoming apparent. Some other things were said and I sensed

JUNE 25: TRAINING, DAY 4

a frustration in communication which must be dealt with every day by those who are deaf. In a few short moments the plight of the deaf became apparent. While the blind are cut off from nature, from seeing the mountains, the trees, the rivers; the deaf are cut off from people. They are cut off from the whispering, background noises and discussions that go into making decisions and many of the processes of leadership and authority acceptance.

A potential erosion was occurring in my ability to move the team rapidly if needed. I was getting tired, felt powerless, angered and a little sad because I knew other moments would occur because of the need to be able to make decisions and change plans rapidly as a mountain requires. Mountains are not static. They move, creak, hiss, rumble and give off many signals that we hear, sometimes with a virtual inner ear. After twenty-five years of climbing and guiding I knew that acknowledging and accepting the decision of the leader could mean the difference between life and death. The recent tragedy on Rainier only heightened my sense of concern.

Alec and Paul would probably feel like a yo-yo jerked in one direction and then in another by some of the decisions that would be made as circumstances changed on the mountain. Every effort would have to be made to make sure that Chuck, Fitz, and Rich could interpret during group meetings. For the time being I explained the situation to Fitz and asked him to intercede if necessary. I wasn't sure I would be able to communicate with Alec or Paul, who were starting to act out their frustrations, and I didn't want to drop them from the team. I did tell them both that if they wanted I would pay for their return flight home if they were not going to cooperate. Wounds had been inflicted that would not heal.

We headed for Independence Pass. Two miles west of the Pass there is a curve with a wide shoulder and space to park. A mountain stream cascades down from a valley to the north and passes under the highway through a culvert. The cars were parked alongside the stream. While still alongside the road Fitz started a dinner of beef stroganoff, Judy made salad, and I scouted the trails on both sides of the river for flat ground where we could sleep. Five minutes from the cars I found a suitable area large enough for all the tents.

After dinner it was decided not to set up the tents. The cumulus clouds that had built up during the afternoon, although threatening, looked as if they would dissipate. For several it was the first time they had slept in the open with stars for a ceiling, and the only sound was from the river twenty feet away. Everybody was tired and full. Kirk later said he was asleep before he hit the ground.

CHAPTER 6

JUNE 26: TRAINING, DAY 5

The ridges above the 12,095-foot pass blocked the morning sun and there was a chill in the camping area. Doug crawled out of his sleeping bag and put on his boots, stretched looking nowhere in particular, and called out, "Phil."

When I answered he walked to me and said quietly, "When we're through with this trip remind me to say something about last night." He was finding the physical effort demanding and was having doubts about his ability to make the climb. As he learned more about climbing techniques and requirements he began to understand the nature of the potential risk he was undertaking. The Rainier tragedy was bothering him. He had decided he would not climb the mountain but would continue practicing and not say anything until the last minute.

The sleeping bags were draped on the wild blueberry and mountain laurel bushes to let the dew dry off while a breakfast of French toast, pancakes, coffee and hot chocolate was consumed. The film crew had spent the night in Aspen and had arrived in time for pancakes. They brought a newspaper with an article by Tim Egan, a PI (Post

Intelligencer) and NY Times reporter from Seattle. Tim had spent the first day at Buckskin Pass and had already returned to Seattle. The team enjoyed its first taste of public recognition.

The plan for the day was to climb to the top of a 13,000- foot ridge to the south of Independence Pass. The sky was blue and clear as the party set off from the Pass. Some cumuli were building to the west and east heralding the beginning of another daily cycle of cloud building.

During the day the sun warms the air and the ground and melts the snow. The warmer air absorbs moisture from the ground and rises. As the warm, moist air rises to the higher altitudes, it cools and clouds form. Because of the snow pack and cold ground from the winter and the strength of the spring sun, the cloud building process can be rapid and generate violent thunderstorms. We hiked half a mile before getting out of sight of our cars and away from the sounds of the occasional vehicle going over the pass.

The Pass is well above timberline and there were no trees or bushes. A carpet of grasses, moss, and a myriad of yellow, white, blue and red alpine flowers made traveling easy. At one point the film crew had run ahead over a knoll and was expecting the Pelion team to come over the knoll in single file. I used the moment to have a little fun and to encourage a greater level of exertion. Pulling the team together I suggested they spread out and we all charge broadside at the same time. Everybody liked the idea and we crawled to the edge of the knoll. At an agreed upon signal everybody jumped up and charged onto the camera crew, running unguided like a bunch of wild Indians

JUNE 26: TRAINING, DAY 5

whooping and hollering. They ran as hard as they could across the open, flower-covered meadow with nothing to bump into but a camera crew.

The run, with packs on near 13,000 feet had everyone's hearts and lungs pumping hard. They stopped to catch their breath. Some sat down and said they couldn't move anymore; others flopped on the ground with their arms spread out.

After resting we regrouped and roped up in teams of five to practice team travel and to hike to the top of the ridge. I told them I wanted them to travel for two hours without stopping.

The cumuli were developing more rapidly than they had all week, and in the distance the bottoms of the clouds were turning black. The teams moved uphill in a long single file. Nearly everybody was moving with a much steadier pace than two days before. They stomped a foot down with each resting step and exhaled each breath forcefully.

Justin still appeared unfocused in his walking and seemed to amble along without the rhythm of the rest step and without the resting, momentary relaxing pause of the forward leg. Judy appeared weak and hung on the rope, letting the person in front pull her along.

We met two elderly ladies who were coming down the hill. As they passed, one of the ladies asked, "What are you doing here with those black clouds up there?" I had been watching the clouds and assured them we would turn around if conditions got worse. One resident from

Aspen who was along for the day said there was seldom lightning in the Spring, but in the Fall the storms could be quite severe.

Thirty minutes later the first team had reached a flat spot on the ridge and was starting down the backside. The second team was traveling across the flat and a third team was still climbing up. Rick Ridgeway and I saw the same jagged yellow line arc from a black cloud to the ground two ridges to the west. Lightning! So much for local lore on the weather. We were witnessing the one thing we could not control with training, equipment and experience--the weather. Would the weather be a factor on Rainier?

Lightning on a mountain is a spectacular display of raw energy. Lightning striking a peak can travel down the slopes like water down a river bed. Climbers caught in thunderstorms sometimes died in a petrified position as if they had been turned to stone. Others get knocked down the side of the mountain, burned and paralyzed. One acquaintance a number of years before had survived after being caught in a storm. His partner was killed. The climber who had lived had managed to drag himself, burned and half-paralyzed, for nine miles in three days before a search party found him.

In a non-fatal incident a number of years before on a glacier in Alaska I had stepped out of the tent several of us were in and encountered a blank grey horizon. Visibility was about fifty feet. The buttons on my rain coat started buzzing and water droplets danced on their metal surface.

JUNE 26: TRAINING, DAY 5

We were in the middle of an electrical cloud and remained there for the entire day. We moved all metal climbing equipment away from the tent. Amusing but disconcerting was the experience of unzipping my fly and having electrical discharges jump across the zipper. The electrical charge eventually dissipated in three deafening bolts onto an iron and nickel rock outcrop, called a Nunatak, a hundred yards away and a hundred feet higher.

With these experiences vividly in mind I called a retreat of the Pelion team and headed them on a run back down the ridge toward the cars. The blind were told where the obstacles were and where the edge of the ridge was in a constant staccato of instructions. They ran from a crouched position. They extended a leg, planted the foot firmly, and then moved forward keeping the leg bent. This prevented them from twisting an ankle and kept their center of gravity as low as possible.

The pace left little room for error in instructions and no room for complaints about the need for a rest. We traveled at a near-running pace for thirty-five minutes, stretching the time they had been marching without stopping to more than two hours. It was evident that the blind members could move in a strong coordinated team effort under pressure.

As we reached the cars, the first drops of rain fell. The ropes were coiled and the cars repacked. Ridgeway had turned his sleeping pad into a huge sign, "RAINIER OR BUST," and taped it to Big Blue for the trip back to Aspen. We were through with this phase of training. With the exception of Judy, everybody looked like they were ready for Rainier.

Judy's frailty from her "brittle" diabetes, a term used to describe difficulty in maintaining blood sugar stability, could not be ignored. While she seemed to barely hold her own going up, she was now visibly distressed. On the descent I had to support her nearly all the way down. When we reached the cars Fitz drew a blood sample to make a blood sugar measurement. Expecting to find it low, he was surprised to find it instead elevated.

Several members had already expressed concern about Judy's lack of strength and were afraid she would hurt their chances for the summit. I had made allusion to the fact that I would not jeopardize a person's health or the safety of the team. I felt the time to make decisions about the summit team would be just before the summit climb. My hope was that events could be shaped appropriately so as to allow the hard decisions to evolve naturally.

We returned to the St. Moritz and everybody set about repacking and getting ready for the trip to Denver the next morning. I received a call from Dianne. She had talked to Jim. Rainier was in beautiful shape, and the Ingraham looked safe. The search for the eleven climbers caught in the ice fall five days earlier had been called off. They were buried too deep to be found.

JUNE 26: TRAINING, DAY 5

The effects of the five days of training were evident. Everybody felt confident. They felt they had accomplished something and were eager to get on with the climb. Strengths and weaknesses had been identified. Pelion had been forged into a team. And we had the go-ahead to climb Rainier.

CHAPTER 7

JUNE 27, 28 ONWARD TO MT. RAINIER

Before leaving Aspen for Denver the Pelion team had breakfast at 10:00 with the Mayor of Aspen and members of the Chamber of Commerce at the Jerome Hotel. This was the first formal recognition of Pelion and a suggestion of its impact and its stimulating effect on others.

The drive back to Denver was different than the drive to Aspen. There were lively discussions, comparisons of what we had been doing for the past few days and what we might find on Rainier. The banter passed between the two vehicles using the Handi-Talkies on loan from Motorola.

Bud Keith was dropped off in Alta to meet Olaf Pedersen, founder of the Ski For Light skiing programs for the blind. They would later rendezvous with us in Denver. Friends of Judy in Denver, the Eklunds, barbecued steak for dinner and let us camp in their back yard for the night. Nan Eklund had breakfast going before most people were awake. I had the feeling that everybody enjoyed a couple of well cooked meals without having to work them off by carrying a heavy pack all day. The immediate agenda was to get to the airport, fly to Los Angeles, and then to Seattle.

PELION

The ticketing and bag check-in at the airport was a major production. We had thirteen members of the climbing team and a four-person camera crew. Each person had personal gear, a climbing pack and a bag full of general climbing equipment. Fred organized an eight-man relay line and all the bags were moved from the curb from person to person to behind the ticketing counter in a matter of a few minutes. When we left, several attendants were staring at a pile of over 120 packs and boxes, anticipating having to move them to the plane. We tipped them $2.00 a bag and they seemed pleased.

Western Airlines was contributing the air transportation for the team to Colorado, from Colorado to Seattle and then home. The flight to Seattle was by way of Los Angeles. During the short stopover, Rick Ridgeway met Diane Baker, an actress-turned-producer and owner of Artemis Productions, who was making the documentary of the climb. Rick dropped off the movie film taken over the past several days. Dianne Baker had already reviewed the film taken from the first day on the Snowmass-Maroon Bells Trail and thought it looked good.

The flight from Los Angeles to Seattle passed quickly. The sighted members of the party described the scenery and points of interest to the blind members. Mt. Shasta and Mt. Whitney stood out on the clear day. Rick Ridgeway, who was a powerful and accomplished rock climber, pointed out Half Dome and other major climbs in Yosemite. Rick was a talented film maker, writer, lecturer and a strong, experienced mountaineer. He was one of the first Americans to stand on the summit of K2, the second highest mountain in the world. He said he got his start in film making working with Clint Eastwood on the

JUNE 27, 28 ONWARD TO MT. RAINIER

film, "The Eiger Sanction." His job had been to kick rocks off a cliff for sound effects.

Since then he had traveled and made films in the Antarctic, the Himalayas, South America, and the United States. He had climbed the highest peak on each continent and written several books on his adventures.

The plane passed over Crater Lake in southern Oregon and Mt. Hood, east of Portland, where a number of people had been killed in an avalanche the week before. Further north we could see puffs of steam coming from the crater of Mt. St. Helens which had erupted a year before. I had flown over St. Helens the day before it erupted and was climbing north of Mt. Rainier when St. Helens blew 50 million tons of rock and ash into the air. Now the crater opened to the northeast onto hundreds of square miles of forest that had been decimated and lay in a mat of brown and grey.

The fan-shaped pattern of waste stretched toward Mt. Rainier. The symmetrical dome of the Mt. Adams volcano was to the east. The Olympic Mountains on the west and the Cascades to the east were dwarfed by the massiveness of Rainier.

Dave Nickolson, a friend who would be helping us on Rainier, and a team of four skiers had been near 9,000 feet on Rainier when St Helens, forty miles away erupted. What they witnessed was incomprehensible. Within moments they had seen the ash cloud spreading toward them. At 9,000 feet there is nothing to block the view between the peaks.

They saw the ridges of the lesser mountains between the two volcanic giants disappearing as the black cloud expanded. Recovering from their moment of shock, they turned their skis downward and hurried to get to their cars five miles down the slopes before the cloud got to them.

They were professional skiers and spared few tricks in making the descent. The first mile-and-half dropped away rapidly as they descended at speeds in excess of fifty miles an hour. The air started filling with a fine, nearly invisible grey powder. They raced on, nearly choking in the advancing cloud of ash. The surface of the snow turned a light grey and their skis started grabbing at the pumice film that was accumulating. Within moments the descent halted as the smooth surface of snow turned into a crusty sheet of sandpaper. They released their bindings and covered their mouths with handkerchiefs to filter out the ash as they tried to breathe and ran, then walked as fast as they could down the last mile to their cars and escaped.

When we landed at SEA-TAC airport the other passengers disembarked. Jim Whittaker and Dianne Roberts came aboard and welcomed us to Seattle. Jim told us that the press was outside in the lobby and that we would spend time with them while we waited for luggage.

The reception area was jammed with reporters, photographers, TV cameras, floodlights, spectators, family members and friends. Richard Rose's wife and son, Paul Stefurak's wife, Sheila's mother and other supporters were in the crowd. Richard's mother-in-law had knitted

JUNE 27, 28 ONWARD TO MT. RAINIER

wool hats for each team member and brought fresh strawberries and cherries.

I met my brother, Jeff, to pick up two flags to carry to the summit: an American flag that had flown over the capitol in Washington, D.C., and a United Nations flag recognizing the International Year of Disabled Persons (IYDP). Jeff also had a box of 500 granola bars, a hundred packages of breakfast squares and a dozen boxes of Bisquick from General Mills.

My youngest son Christopher, who lived in Seattle, arrived and gave me a bag of jelly beans to carry to the summit.

Several vehicles and a small bus were used to carry the large pile of equipment and people to Mt. Rainier National Park. While the assortment of 120 packs, suitcases and boxes was being loaded, everybody ate fresh strawberries and cherries.

SEA-TAC airport is ninety miles from the west side entrance to Mt. Rainier National Park. The closer we traveled to the mountain, the bigger it appeared until it loomed over the landscape and completely dominated the skyline. We reached the park entrance around seven o'clock. The small caravan stopped at the Longmire Hiker's Center, ten miles in from the entrance to stretch, breathe fresh mountain air and to explore the mountain.

In the Hiker's Center there was a large relief' model of the mountain. The film crew set up lights and cameras. As circumstances will happen, out of the 120 original bags, only one was misplaced…the one with the keys to the camera box. While Bob Carmichael, the cameraman located a bolt cutter to remove the lock, the rest of us took off in different directions. Some of the team listened to a lecture on beavers.

Judy, Bud, Rich and I took a walk along the Longmire woodland nature trail. Judy and Bud had never experienced a large skunk cabbage, or a forest with a wall-to-wall, two-inch-thick carpet of moss; or hemlock trees five feet in diameter; or trillium and a variety of delicate ferns; or the armor of needles on Devil's Club that grow in the twilight of the forest. Each of these was found by gentle touching, sometimes on hands and knees. The final step from the Paradise woodland trail onto the asphalt led back to the reality of the Rainier model.

The model of the mountain was eight feet square and stood nearly two feet high with a summit crater about three inches in diameter. It highlights the major ridges, glacier, cliffs, and surrounding peaks. For several of the blind climbers this was their first encounter with the shape of a mountain. Fred thought a volcanic mountain would be a smooth cone and was surprised by the rugged, irregular contours and the twisted cascading shape of the glaciers revealed at his touch.

Mt. Rainier National Park was established in 1899. It encompasses an area of 378 square miles. The park has the largest glacier system in the continental United States with 26 glaciers and 35 square miles of ice. Rainier is the highest of six volcanic peaks in the state of Washington. Because of its 14,410-foot height, it disturbs the flow of moist air coming from the Pacific Ocean, resulting in a great deal of snow and a variety of cloud formations. High winds moving over the mountain form

JUNE 27, 28 ONWARD TO MT. RAINIER

a cloud that hovers over the summit like a cap. Sometimes high winds cause a line of saucer-shaped lenticular clouds to trail out behind the mountain for a hundred miles.

Those who were blind explored the model with their fingers and were shown the route they would climb. For forty-five minutes they ran their fingers over the mountain, the glaciers, rivers and foothills. At times there were ten hands on the summit.

"Where is the route?"
"What is this steep section?" "Is this a glacier?"

Mt RAINIER

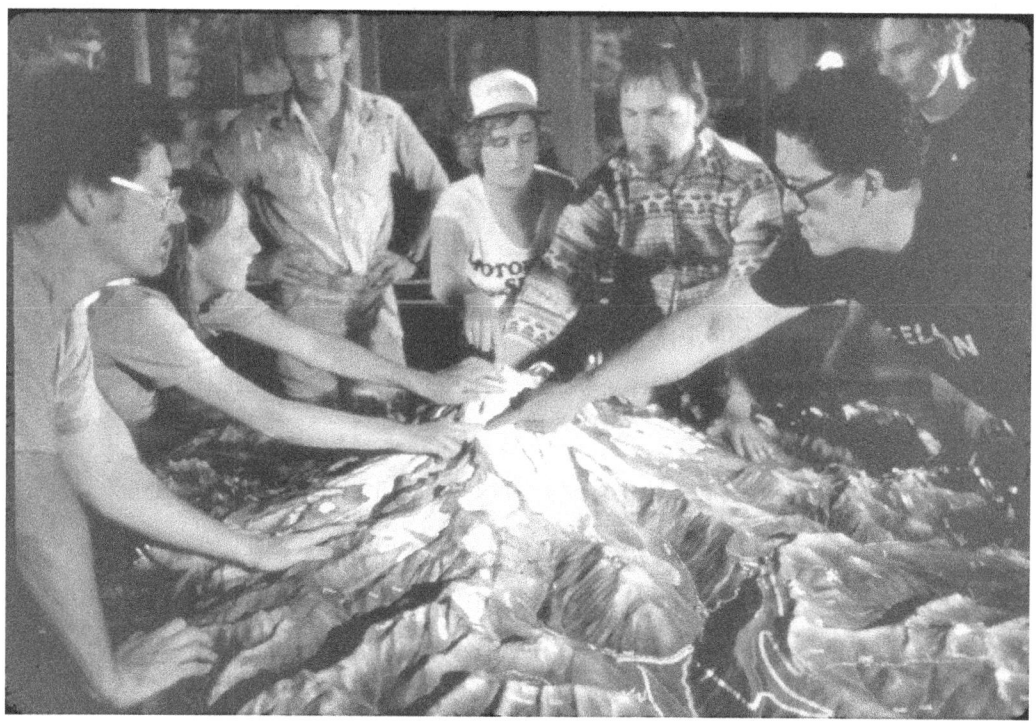

The first view of the mountain.

"Where am I now?"

"How far is it from here, (pointing with one finger) to here?" (indicating with the other hand.)

They would get lost and disoriented and wanted to know where they were. Sheila put a finger on the depression of the crater asking, "What's this?"

Jim answered, "The summit, you're on top."

She responded, "Gee, and I'm not even tired."

Now they were starting to understand why I had chosen Rainier. It offered long expanses of unobstructed travel, had a minimum of rock fall and was the biggest thing in the country that could be done safely. I could already imagine the warmth of sun and the coolness of the glacier, and smell the mingled aromas of sweat and sun cream after hours of continuous uphill climbing.

Outside the sun was setting on the mountain summit nearly 11,000 feet above our position. The caravan continued on to Paradise Lodge, another thirteen miles up the road. Half-way to Paradise we crossed a bridge over the roaring milky-white-and-brown Nisqually River.

When I first climbed Rainier thirty years before, the leading edge of the Nisqually Glacier came within a half-mile of the bridge. As the glacier has melted over the years it has shrunk and retreated up the mountain out of sight behind a bend in the dirt cliffs, leaving a boulder-strewn river bed. The cliffs lining the river are composed of boulders of every size,

JUNE 27, 28 ONWARD TO MT. RAINIER

from golf balls to some larger than cars, held together with compacted silica flour ground from the basalt bedrock as the glacier advanced.

The river turns white as it erodes away the grey matrix holding the rocks. The rocks released from the binding material roll loose and crash into the river, leaving pock marks in the wall which in turn crumble into a dusty cloud. As we drove over the bridge a hundred feet above, the thumping of large rocks rolling into the stream bed could be heard over the roar of the water.

The road climbs at a steep angle along the forested side of the lesser mountain range. A low rock wall serves as the barrier between the road and a thousand-foot abyss. A mile up the road from the bridge a huge, brown-colored bear climbed over the retaining wall on the right, lumbered in front of the bus, climbed up the steep bank on the left and disappeared into the woods. The powerful animal seemed like an omen of strength and nature's way of blessing our trip.

Paradise Lodge, built in 1917, is an enormous log cabin. The lobby is dominated by pillars and rafters made with two and three-foot-diameter logs. Massive fireplaces at both ends are used as gathering places in the evening and a place to dry out on rainy days. Once at the lodge everyone settled into their rooms quickly.

Fitz and I visited a radio relay trailer in the parking lot. The Motorola Corporation had installed a radio repeater tower on it to make sure that communications could be maintained with us during the climb. The trailer would also be the central communications and information center for the press and spectators.

It was cold and the bright stars outlined the Tatoosh range to the west and the mountain to the east. As Fitz and I hiked back to the lodge, I described the hassle I'd had with the Federal Communications Commission in getting a license and authority to operate the repeater tower. It had taken over two months of paper work and phone calls. In effect we would be operating a radio station, and I had to fill out an application for a license which included a description of the broadcast facility, the purpose of the station, the power of the station and the exact location of the tower in terms of latitude, longitude and altitude.

Fitz went to bed and I spent the better part of the night sorting out food and equipment. The second floor corridor in the lodge staff area became an assembly station. Each of the three meals a day for twenty to twenty-six people for the next six to seven days was set out in piles the length of the hall.

For each day there was a pile of Kool Aid packets; lettuce, cucumbers and tomatoes for a salad; two large sausages, two or three blocks of cheese and Triscuits for lunch; dehydrated dinners; Bisquick, eggs, coffee and hot chocolate mixes for breakfast. Pots, pans, stoves, white gas lanterns, ropes and miscellaneous items were put in other piles. The food for each meal was packed in large bags and labeled-- "Mon.Brk.", "Mon.Lnch.", "Mon.Din."...When there seemed to be some semblance of order I went to bed. The remaining details of organization could be handled in the morning before the major ceremonies.

CHAPTER 8

JUNE 29 MT. RAINIER, DAY 1

It was a cool, crisp morning as the team walked the quarter of a mile from the lodge down to the Visitors Center. The valleys were clear and the distant skies were blue. Moisture-laden winds hitting the peak were forced upward into the colder altitudes, causing condensation and the formation of a cloud cover that obscured Rainier's summit. It was ten o'clock and a large crowd was gathering outside the Visitors Center, lending a feeling of parade and pageantry. The climbers lined up in a semi-circle in front of a brazier filled with hot coals. Their packs were either on the ground or on benches behind them.

I felt a sense of relief. I had been frantically busy since six ice axes and other equipment that had been originally lost in shipment to Aspen had to be borrowed from the Guide Service, which did not open until 9:00 AM. Arrangements had been made with the Guide Service to conduct a glacier training program the next day.

I had to find Harold Krentz to give him the flags for the ceremony. Arrangements had to be made with ten to fifteen people to serve as porters to help carry equipment to high camp. I had run back and forth among the breakfast tables in the restaurant, the Guide Shack, the assembly area, and the lobby. At that point I felt as if climbing the mountain was going to be the easy part.

Jerry Tayes of the National Park Service introduced the team to the bystanders. Ralph Munro, Secretary of the Washington Department of State presented the team with a State flag to carry to the summit. Mr. Munro introduced Harold Krentz, representing the White House, who presented the team with the American and the U.N. IYDP flags.

Harold, blind since birth, expressed his feelings about the challenge of Pelion by singing a number of verses from songs he had written for the Broadway play, "Butterflies Are Free" which was based on his life. Later that evening he would give a small concert for the people at Paradise Lodge.

When Harold finished singing, Joe Washington, a Lummi Indian Medicine Man was introduced. I had met Joe a couple of years before while trying to develop an outdoor challenge program for teenagers on the Lummi Indian Nation. When planning Pelion I had asked Joe if he could help us by providing a Safe Journey Ceremony.

Joe was a big person physically and spiritually. A fisherman by trade, his skin was weathered by the many years on the salt water of Puget Sound and the San Juan Straits of northwestern Washington. Now in his seventies he devoted most of his efforts to trying to maintain both tribal and spiritual customs. When Indian spiritual leaders from other Nations gathered, Joe was often asked to be their leader and to open ceremonies.

JUNE 29 MT. RAINIER, DAY 1

Pressed up by a beaded head band holding three eagle feathers, Joe Washington's white hair looked like a halo. He wore a red shirt and a long buckskin vest with beaded shields on his chest, and strings of beads around his neck. His rawhide belt held pouches of herbs and medicines.

He greeted each of us and pressed a circle of red "Sacred Earth" paint onto our cheekbones with his thumbs. He said it was important to leave the paint there and not wash it off because it offered protection. As he explained to the crowd the meaning of the paint, he placed grasses and other medicine into the brazier of coals. As part of the ceremony he handed me a medicine staff holding four eagle feathers which were mounted using beads so that the feathers could catch the wind and dance. The slightest breath of air, even that caused by the draft of a moving hand would stir the feathers. He told me the medicine staff was to be placed on the summit.

Joe picked up a hand drum with a thin brown animal skin stretched over a circular wooden frame, burnished from years of ceremonial use. His hands brushed the drum generating a low rumble while he chanted to the mountain and earth. Then he put the drum down and only the wind could be heard.

Joe then sprinkled water on a rattle of gourds and flower seedpods and began to sing as he moved to each person. Magic was in his song, or for those who don't believe, there were moments of interesting circumstances. As Joe sang, the clouds over the summit dissipated. When he stopped singing to sprinkle more water on the rattle, the clouds again covered the mountain.

PELION

Joe Washington, Lummi Tribe

Joe greeting and blessing Jim Whittaker

Media and well-wishers at Safe Journey ceremony.

Joe Washington explaining the Journey

JUNE 29 MT. RAINIER, DAY 1

Joe Washington singing and clearing clouds from the mountain.

Joe Washington Instructing Phil on the ceremony for the summit

When he renewed his chant the clouds parted again, revealing a brilliant, snow-covered summit with a blue sky as background. Each time Joe stopped singing the clouds tried to return. When Joe Washington finally stopped, there was a brilliant, clear blue sky. One small cloud, shaped like a feather, sparkled the colors of the rainbow.

Technicolor eagle feather over the Tatoosh Range.

Chills ran up some of the team's spines. Alec passed out face down on the ground in front of the brazier. Fitz went over to help revive him. Joe gave each of the climbers some Indian medicine to put onto the fire. The blind were guided to the brazier so they would not be burned while making their offerings. Gayle Eversole, a long-time friend of mine, who had driven Joe from his home on the Lummi reservation to Rainier, handed me a medicine pouch. Joe placed some of the medicines and sweet grass charred in another part of the ceremony into the pouch to make a medicine bundle. I was instructed that when we reached the summit, I was to offer some of the contents of the bundle to the four directions, to the heavens, and to the earth.

JUNE 29 MT. RAINIER, DAY 1

Joe sang as everybody put their packs put on. With eagle feathers in hand and with Jim Whittaker at my side, I led the climbers out of the Visitor's Center concourse to a trail heading up the mountain. Photographers and TV cameramen ran ahead and walked backwards taking pictures, or walked alongside taking pictures, trampling delicate alpine flowers. A quarter of a mile up the trail Jim stopped the group so they could fill their water bottles, adjust boots and take off some of the warmer clothing in which they had started the day.

While the group relaxed Jim and I ran down to the Lodge for some food and miscellaneous items that had been left aside in order to get the ceremony started on schedule. We returned with the additional supplies to meet the team, which had grown in size to twenty. We were the eleven disabled, myself, Fitz, Dianne Roberts, Jim, the four on the film crew and Dave Nickolson, one of my high school climbing partners who was going to help with glacier practice the next day.

Breathing deeply and using the rest step, the train of pack-laden climbers slowly made its way up the trail.

We started uphill one step at a time which is the only way to climb a mountain.

The trail was steep, the packs were heavy and legs were a little stiff. With each step I could feel gravity trying to pull me backwards. Right foot...breathe. Left foot...breathe. Non-stop. Right foot...breathe. Left foot...breathe. I commented to Doug, "It is impossible to start slow enough," then to the others, "Take it easy until your body warms up then you can stretch out your step and increase your pace. Warm up first."

Each blind person hung onto the pack of the sighted person in front. We traveled an hour before stopping to rest, then continued up another forty minutes to a point where we could climb down onto the Nisqually glacier, three hundred feet below. The Nisqually is still a large glacier but has only a fraction of its former mass. It used to fill the whole valley three-quarters of a mile across and three hundred feet higher. As the glacier melted over the years its depth decreased and there was not enough glacial mass to push into the valley. Now the lower end of the glacier is covered with dirt and boulders. Its crevasses are shallow and their

Climbing from Paradise Lodge

JUNE 29 MT. RAINIER, DAY 1

Heading toward the Nisqually Glacier

edges rounded by the sun and rain. This was the first time the team was on steep snow with packs. We were going downhill which is more difficult than going up. A slip could send a person to the bottom.

I remembered that this was the first slope I had ever been on with skis. That was a long time ago. We had intended to ski on the glacier and had to get down the slope. It was the steepest thing I could imagine. The fellow in front of me slipped and disappeared over the rounded slope, so steep it was not possible to see where the slope connected with the bottom. A minute later he reappeared sliding across the flat at the bottom, head first on his back. I could still remember the numbing sensation from the adrenalin I felt, not wanting to fall.

In order to maintain balance while going down a slope it is necessary to bend the knees and crouch before extending a foot down. Even without a pack it can be difficult. With a pack on, the thigh muscles are tensed and tire rapidly because this is a leg movement that is seldom used. The closest similar action is walking down stairs two at a time slowly, without jumping. Movement was now cautious as the blind climbers crouched and searched for footing, or stomped steps into the hard surface, moving diagonally down the hill to the lateral moraine.

A moraine is a pile of rocks and dirt carried down the mountain on the sides of the glacier. Rainier was formed through volcanic activity and much of the rock is dark reddish brown, relatively soft basalt that weathers easily. The tops of the ridges and cliffs, left by the carving action of the glacier as it scoured its valley under the pull of gravity, are covered with a loose blanket of debris of weathered red boulders and dirt. Winter's snows and frost action push the debris over the edge. More is washed down by rain or melted free from the frozen grip of ice by the sun.

On stormy days thousands of rivulets and gullies carry red slurry of volcanic debris onto the glacier's edge. On sunny days boulders melt loose, fall, and break into smaller boulders and clouds of basalt dust as they smash on the piles of rock and talus on the side of the glacier lining the base of the cliffs.

As the glacier grinds and carves into the rotten walls and bed rock, its edges are covered with the debris cascading down. When the glacier stagnates, dies, or retreats after several years of low snowfall and warm weather and the ice melts, the rocks remain, forming a ridge parallel to the glacier. The rocks that were pushed along by the bulldozer action of the front of the glacier form the terminal moraine after the glacier melts.

The lateral moraine is formed by the rocks dropped onto the edge of the glacier. Lateral moraines can serve as a form of fingerprint which distinguishes the glacier's flow. In Alaska, where many glaciers flow together like tributaries into a river, the lateral moraines slide together on the side where the glaciers meet, forming a ribbon of rock in the middle of the combined glacier. As more glaciers merge, more ribbons form. A large glacier viewed from the air can take on the pattern of a woven Indian blanket.

It took forty minutes for the team to descend to a hundred-foot-wide flat area between the valley wall and the moraine. There, amidst yodeling, the infamous Whittaker moose call, and shouts of, "What do I do now?" platforms were dug from the snow and tents were set up. The blind team members could not be distinguished from the sighted among the tasks.

Tents were removed from packs. The fiberglass tent pole sections were connected to make a fifteen-foot rod that was fed through the guides running over the surface of the hemisphere-shaped dome tents. Three sets of poles were used on each tent. The ends of the flexible rods attached to clips on the outer edge of the tent floor, stretching the top of the dome taut. The rounded shape of the tent provides resistance to strong winds and allows head room for sitting.

Sheila and Kirk setting up a tent **Sheila helping Alec**

Once camp was established Jim led the group up onto the snow-covered moraine ridge to practice the rest step and self-arrest, techniques we had practiced at Buckskin Pass in Colorado. When Jim started to explain the concepts he held his ice axe in the air and said, "OK, gang, here is how we hold our ice axe."

Dianne said, "Jim, they can't see you."

The snow slope was longer than the one at Buckskin Pass and there was no drop-off at the bottom. Here the climbers could push themselves off the top and slide down the steep slope until they stopped. After a couple of trips down, sitting and going feet first, Jim had them lie on their backs and slide down head first, then try to stop their descent. The seriousness of the training evaporated into a contest to see who could slide the furthest out onto the flat at the bottom of the ridge. I

JUNE 29 MT. RAINIER, DAY 1

think Fitz won with Sheila a close second. Besides just sliding like a bunch of kids with new

Camp on the glacial moraine

Sheila finger spelling with Paul

Jim and Phil leading Pelion team onto the glacier

Jim instructing team on self-arrest technique

sleds, they practiced stopping themselves with the ice axe in the self-arrest position by digging their toes into the snow and pushing their chests down onto their ice axes to drive the pick into the snow.

An important part of the play activity was to get used to getting into the self-arrest from any awkward position they might be in should they fall. The self-arrest has to be a coordinated reflex action. A climber falling on steep snow or ice can slide a long way if he does not react immediately. As with every other task of the past week strengths and weaknesses were observed. Two hours of daylight remained.

Chuck O'Brien demonstrating the self-arrest.

JUNE 29 MT. RAINIER, DAY 1

When we regrouped we set out for some glacier experience. We organized teams of three people to a rope then walked up the moraine to find an easy path onto the glacier.

Some ravens had been hopping around on the snow where we were hiking and had left large tracks. Fred and several of the others were able to gently feel the deep prints before they melted under their touch. After a short hike of several hundred yards, "Pelion" walked onto glacial snow and ice for the first time.

Fred being shown bird tracks in the snow

We crossed a number of small crevasses near the edge of the glacier. Glaciers are rivers of ice tumbling, crashing and flowing to the valley below in frozen slow motion. They can advance five to six inches a year, break into towers of ice, and crack forming crevasses which later fuse together in a plastic flow as they move around ridges or over rocks and cliffs of the mountain underneath. Crevasses can be hundreds of feet deep in places.

Crevasses also can be a fraction of an inch wide and fifty to two hundred feet deep. They can open during the day and close at night. They can also be as wide as they are deep. Some are wide at the top with sides that taper downward to form a V shape over a hundred feet deep. If the bottom of the glacier is being forced up over a ridge the crevasse can be wide at the bottom with only a thin crack or no sign at all on the top. The surface of the glacier can be a thin roof over a crevasse.

An unsuspecting climber can step through the fragile veil of ice and fall into a widening chasm with no hope except for his rope and an alert partner. The walls of crevasses in less turbulent areas sometimes show the annual layers of winter snow, each of which is covered by the dirt and dust of summer.

The top of the glacier we stepped onto was still covered with winter's snow which was solidifying in a cycle of melting during the day and refreezing at night. This process changes the snow into a crust of larger crystals. Footsteps on this surface sound different as the snow changes. A person familiar with the environment can almost subconsciously detect crevasses beneath.

JUNE 29 MT. RAINIER, DAY 1

In the morning the snow would be solid and then soften in the afternoon sun. As we walked toward the center of the glacier, a blind climber occasionally stepped into a small crevasse and fell in up to his or her waist. Even sighted climbers occasionally stepped on a crusty shell of snow and broke through to the crevasse below. It was apparent that ropes and teamwork were necessary for safety.

From time to time the quiet mountain air reverberated with booming, rattling sounds. Some of the sounds came from avalanches higher up. Other noises came from ice-bound rocks melting loose from the cliffs on the other side of the glacier as they rattled, clattered and boomed onto the boulder pile lining the side of the glacier. Most of the glacier was covered with fresh snow from the storms of the past week.

Islands of dark, clear ice rose up in places. This was centuries-old ice that had been reshaped many times in its journey from higher on the mountain to the quiet flow it experienced now. Jim led the rope teams to one of the outcroppings for a brief exploration of its structure before returning to camp.

We planned to practice more technical glacier techniques in the morning. Fred said, "I thought glaciers were a smooth piece of ice, like a tilted, frozen pond. This is lumpy, rolling, rough, and alive."

These raised outcropping islands were covered with rocks and dirt, and the ice was so hard it was difficult to chop a footstep into it even with an ice axe. Rivulets of water ran down the nearly-impenetrable surface, filling some of the smaller crevasses.

Back in camp Jim crawled into his tent and lit the stoves for coffee water and dinner. I mixed up a pot of dehydrated beef stroganoff for twenty-one hungry people. Most of the team spread their sleeping bags out inside their tents and rested until dinner was ready. Fred hiked to a rock outcropping to fill canteens from a small rivulet of water formed by the melting snow on the upper slopes. During the night the water would stop flowing.

As we ate, the sun dropped behind the Tatoosh range to the west. The slopes around camp turned grey and an invisible river of cold air flowed down the mountain and glacier, and through our camp. High above us the mountain glowed orange, then pink under the last rays of sunlight. The sun set and the mountain towered over us as a giant white ghost against a darkening sky. One or two avalanches crunched into the darkness before the dropping temperatures locked the ice into a suspended state for the night.

Several reporters hovered off to one side while we ate. It was difficult to tell if they were waiting for food or a story. When dinner was finished one of the reporters asked if we had any extra hot water. They didn't have a stove. Reporters from all over the country were trying to follow Pelion. Some, it seemed, had never been off the sands of Florida beaches and now wanted to stomp around on glaciers at high altitude. Many of them had absolutely no idea of the risk to which they were exposing themselves.

A number of the team members commented as they crawled into their tents and sleeping bags that this was the first time they had ever slept on snow. The tent floor was waterproof. We used thin, closed-cell foam rubber mats for insulation and a cushion from the cold, hard snow. Once the tent opening was zipped tight the stream of cold air outside rustled the sides of the tent gently. The inside became a warm cocoon of down sleeping bags. From time to time someone called from one tent to someone in another. Bud reached into his warehouse of jokes.

Perhaps it was the release of the tension of the day, but Bud had me paralyzed with uncontrollable laughter. A voice from Jim's tent suggested that everybody go to sleep. Every day thus far had been filled with first-time experiences, but this day had been exceptional.

CHAPTER 9

JUNE 30 MT. RAINIER, DAY 2

Some time after two in the morning Mother Nature decided to let us know she was still in charge and the clouds drifted in. We awoke on Tuesday to a heavy grey mist that promised to turn to rain. Visibility varied between a hundred feet and fifty feet, depending on how the fog-like low cloud drifted, turning our world into grey mist against a white slope of snow. At times the tents even twenty feet away faded into the grey, blank landscape.

I placed a flat rock to serve as a platform for the stove at the bottom of a hole stomped in the snow. The walls of the hole kept the wind from blowing out the flame. A large box of Bisquick was converted to pancakes and snow was melted for coffee. Everybody put on their heavy parkas and rain slickers as they crawled out of their tents to stand in the mist and eat. After breakfast each climber tied a twenty-five-foot length of one-inch-wide webbing around his waist and thighs to form a swami seat. The swami takes the pressure off the climber's waist and ribs and makes it possible to sit comfortably without the strangling pressure of rope under the ribs if there is a fall. They strapped the metal-framed, spiked crampons onto their boots. Fingers grew numb from the cold, wet metal of the crampons and the buckles of the straps. It felt good to get gloves on after sitting in the snow wrestling with the crampons.

At 10:30 Lou Whittaker, Phil Erschler and Andy Politz from the Rainier Guide Service emerged from the mist like an aura of alien force. The Guides were going to provide their one-day training program gratis. After the devastating, avalanche the previous week's enrollments for climbing dropped. The Pelion activity was a way of signaling that the mountain was safe and the guiding business door was still open.

The guides knew the need for experience with the basics. Phil Erschler had climbed Rainier 250 times over the past eleven years with the Guide Service -- more than any other person. Lou, Jim's twin brother, led us back to the moraine ridge. He was going to start with the basics: how to breathe and how to walk, the same as in Colorado and during the day before. It would still be three days before most of the team really understood the importance of breathing deeply and the rest step.

Lou started to instruct the group on how to hold the ice axe for the self-arrest. He held it above his head in both hands and in a voice loud enough for an auditorium said, "Now here is how we hold the ice axe." Jim, standing to the side was quick to recall the events of the day before and commented, "Lou, they can't see you." A few minutes later, with another sight-oriented instruction like--"Now watch Andy as he..." Jim again reminded Lou that he was talking to blind people.

Lou checked with Jim to verify that the Pelion team knew the self-arrest, the rest step going up, and the plunge step going down the slope.

Lou and his staff roped the Pelion team into groups of three. Then he led them out onto the glacier, and over the crevasses to an outcropping of hard blue-ice. One of the guides anchored one end of a rope at the top of a steep slope and dropped the other end to the bottom. Each climber walked around to the bottom and then, hanging onto the line, worked his or her way to the top.

They all learned to walk on crampons. They learned to walk a little like a penguin, with feet spread apart to avoid accidentally stepping on a boot or catching a spike on a pant leg. They learned how to stomp down hard with a flat-footed jarring thrust to dig all ten points into the ice which was almost as hard as concrete. They had to practice bending their ankles in order to walk upright on a steep slope and still keep all the points of the crampons on the ice. They practiced carefully so they would not step on their own feet with the long spikes. As they practiced, the mist turned to rain.

Judy wasn't able to climb the steeper section. She lost her balance and didn't have the strength to hold herself with the rope. She fell twice and Lou grabbed her each time, and then lowered her to the bottom.

PELION

Two teams of reporters got lost in the fog trying to find Pelion and wandered for several hours before spotting the climbers. From a distance Pelion looked like a group of Technicolor penguins. Team members wore red, green and blue down parkas and red rain suits. When they weren't involved in a specific task they stood with their arms straight down to their sides so water wouldn't get into their sleeves. When they did move they did so with the flat-footed, waddling motion.

The most interesting exercise of the afternoon was a Tyrolean traverse in which the climbers slid fifty feet across a rope stretched over a chasm. Lou Whittaker and Phil Erschler attached both ends of the rope to bollards, which are pillars of snow or ice carved out of the hard glacier ice. To the inexperienced it looked about as secure as hanging from a Popsicle but was in fact rock solid. Everybody in turn was snapped onto the traverse line with a carabineer hooked to their swami belts and then tied onto a belay. While hanging onto the traverse line they got down on hands and knees, then pushed their feet over the lip and slid off the edge of the ice cliff and sat in their swami. When they let go of the line, they slid fifty feet across to the opposite side.

To finish off the day of filming, the camera crew asked Rich Rose to climb the thirty-foot vertical face on the edge of the crevasse which the group had been traversing. Rich was as enthusiastic as anybody could be on such a drizzly day. He wanted to do everything.

Rich had been recommended by the Epilepsy Foundation of America. He was a resident of Washington State and had recently won a major court case against a company that had discriminated against

JUNE 30 MT. RAINIER, DAY 2

him because of his epilepsy. Now he wanted to climb the mountain as a statement about the capabilities of people with epilepsy.

Lou Whittaker belayed as Rich inched his way up the wall of ice and snow on his crampon toe-points and ice axe. At times he would go limp from the struggle, then find extra energy and fight on. It took twenty minutes before he climbed to the top and was over the edge. The camera crew asked him to look heroic and say, "I did it." Rich tried to look serious and quoted his line. He didn't sound convincing. The film crew had him try three more times. Finally Ridgeway said half-heartedly, "OK, that's good, let's go," and the camera crew stopped recording. Rich relaxed and a smile spread across his face which could be seen from across the chasm. He exclaimed, "Hey! I did it, I really did it." With the camera off he provided an Oscar-level performance.

The rope teams headed for camp to repack and return to the lodge for dinner, a good night's sleep and a chance to dry out. After the day of standing in the rain most of the leather boots were wet and cold.

Judy had lost her sight to diabetes nine years before. Not only was she blind but she was also extremely ill in a medical sense. Usually she could control her blood sugar through discipline in diet and the use of insulin. There had been a number of questions about her insulin metabolism even before training started. During the activities in Colorado Judy's blood sugar level was unstable and had varied up and down. Her condition was a constant concern. While others on the trip seemed to get stronger with each day, Judy got weaker. She seemed to be building up, and then would collapse like a rag doll. She responded like a person with low blood sugar when hers was abnormally high.

Judy and Fitz explored the significance of the variations in her sugar levels and other physicians were called and consulted. There didn't seem to be any clear explanations. After the climb I was to find out that she had had hypothalamic ablation surgery in an attempt to save her sight years before and that her body could not develop the level of cortisone necessary to support the level of metabolism required for such a strenuous activity.

Some members of the party were afraid Judy would jeopardize their chances on Rainier and some frictions were developing. While my position as expedition leader was that every attempt would be made to get the whole team to the summit, and that until the summit climb started, nobody would be dropped, it was now time to make the decision. It had become apparent to me in Colorado that Judy would not be able to make the summit, at least not under normal climbing conditions. My hope was that she would learn enough about the demands of the climb to realize the personal risk she would be taking as well as the risk to the rest of the team. A cold, wet day in the mountains has a way of getting people to think more clearly and to become receptive to difficult decisions.

When the team arrived at the Lodge I stopped Jerry Tayes, the Park Ranger working as a liaison with Pelion, to bring him up to date on the condition of the party as we had agreed when Pelion first arrived on the mountain. I explained my concern about Judy; that I would have to ask her to drop out.

Jerry thought he might be able to help. He said that he was mildly diabetic and came from the town next to where Judy lived. The nearness of the town was used as the basis for introducing Judy to Jerry. The three of us talked about Jerry's diabetes and how demanding the mountain was. Judy sensed the direction of the conversation and tears started welling in her eyes. She asked me if I thought she should drop out. Even though I knew the question was coming, it was still disconcerting. There was only one answer, "Yes."

It was a hard decision for Judy. She had been an initial stimulus and mainstay for Pelion. She had worked for a year and a half helping to bring Pelion to reality with the same tough determination that she had put into earning her two graduate degrees and into her professional life. She was not one to give up easily. It was Judy who had made the initial contacts with Western Airlines which provided all the transportation for the team, as well as General Mills. She had written letters to dozens of people seeking their support for the project. None of us would have been on the mountain without the effort she had put into the project.

I held her while she cried. We talked about her decision and the fact that she wasn't giving up on herself, the team, or people with diabetes in general. To do otherwise would be foolhardy. Judy and I walked over to Jim and Lou who were still standing in the lobby. She told them what she had decided. When they put their arms around her and hugged her, she disappeared from view. Both Jim and Lou are 6'5" and she was only 5'3". They shared the burden of her decision and helped her know it was the right one -- and a courageous one. They knew as much as anyone in mountaineering the importance and the difficulty of what she was doing.

Jim and I agreed to get Judy to Camp Muir, and possibly to high camp. She could relay messages on the Handi-Talkies and get coffee water going for when the team returned.

Dinner in the lodge that night was a welcome contrast to sitting on the glacier over a single large pot perched on a rock in a hole in the snow. A number of tables were joined as the whole team sat together at one time. The waitress inadvertently revealed it was her birthday and was struck with embarrassment as seventeen customers spontaneously sang "Happy Birthday."

During dinner Kirk's gregariousness and popularity became obvious. Kirk was young, energetic, handsome, and didn't seem to need eyesight to sense the presence of pretty girls. As the waitress recovered, Kirk asked her if she had gone to high school in Snohomish. She had. They had gone to the same school and he had recognized her voice from the noisy hallway chatter of two years before.

As I paid the dinner bill for the team, I thought how nice it was to have the large check we had received from Philadelphia Life Insurance. Their contribution provided the glue that held many of the project's loose ends together.

Later in the evening I called a group meeting. We crowded into my room. Some members of the team were ritualistically spreading a wax-like snow seal on their boots for waterproofing. Judy let the team know of her decision. For some there was a sense of relief and for others a sense of disappointment.

During the meeting Doug observed that following each beef stroganoff meal the team had gotten wet. First, there was the sprinkler in the park in Aspen; next there was a thunderstorm on Independence Pass; and finally there was the rain on the Nisqually Glacier. After the meeting I checked the food piles to see what we would be eating for the next four days. I removed the beef stroganoff meal intended to be eaten the night before the summit attempt from the packs and put it in the storeroom.

Why take a chance?

CHAPTER 10

JULY 1, MT. RAINIER, DAY 3

Wednesday morning there were low clouds drifting up from the cool valley but the sky above was clear and bright. The team was repacked and dry. After breakfast we assembled outside the lodge before a small crowd of well wishers and press. A brief statement about Judy's decision was made.

Jim reminded the members of the press that they had agreed that they would not interfere with the climb. Even before the trip to Colorado a number of media representatives had expressed interest in climbing with the team. For reasons of safety, some "Protection of documentation investment" and to minimize distractions on the climb, it had been planned that the press could participate during the practice on the glacier. In order to have some coverage two reporters had been invited to climb with the team: Svein Gilje ("Seattle Times") and Tim Egan ("Seattle Post Intelligencer.") Jim finished his statement to the press, then turned to the team and said, "OK gang, the only thing left to do is climb the thing. Let's go."

The weather was perfect; spirits were high; the team was prepared; and everybody knew that the real climb was beginning. Adding to the spirit of determination was a sense of sharing by a number of people who had volunteered one to two days of their time to help carry equipment to Camp Muir and high camp. A couple of park rangers had the day off and volunteered their time. Bud Krogh had contacted a number of people and convinced several of his law partners to come along and help as porters. Five members of a team planning to climb Mt. Everest in 1984 came along to help out. One of the Everest climbers placed a large sign on his pack. The sign read, "Higher the Handicapped."

We started.
Step-rest-breath.
Step-rest-breath.
Step-rest-breath.
Step-rest-breath.

A week and a half of practice was evident as the colorful parade of forty climbers and porters moved like a centipede up the asphalt walks to the snow, past the last stubborn fir trees and blossoming heather to the rocky trails, and finally to one long continuous field of snow. The distance to Camp Muir is only four miles, but it involves a vertical climb of five thousand feet and requires five to eight hours of climbing.

The team stopped only twice for a brief rest and the traditional snacks of climbers- Triscuits, cheese, tuna, granola, breakfast squares, Gorp, juice. In between stops the pace was slow and deliberate, one foot in front of the other. Traveling on the snow was different from hiking on dirt trails. There were no rocks to trip over, but the footing was soft and uneven. One step would be on the surface; on the next step the

JULY 1, MT. RAINIER, DAY 3

surface would break and the climber would punch through up to the knee with a jolt accentuated by the weight of the pack.

The first few climbers formed a small trough in the soft snow which others tried to follow. Steps would be synchronized for awhile. Somehow everybody's right foot would end up in the right foot hole. Every once in a while someone would lose his balance or slip, or do something else to throw off the sequence, and a third foot hole would appear.

Inexperienced climbers sometimes start too fast, go a few hundred yards and slow down, and eventually are passed by those who started slowly. Jim, Dianne and I constantly reminded the climbers to breathe deeply, lock the knee, keep the weight on bone structure not muscle; to go slowly, and keep moving.

The Nisqually glacier is on the left for climbers going up to Camp Muir. At the lodge the whole mountain can be seen. After the first hour the group was five hundred feet higher than they had been when practicing on the glacier. Each additional hour they gained eight to nine hundred feet.

The middle three thousand feet of the Nisqually glacier far below is called the Nisqually Ice Falls. It is a frozen waterfall, a mass of jumbled ice half-a-mile wide, tumbling in slow motion from the summit to the relatively flat part of the Nisqually glacier. Blocks of ice the size of a large house occasionally broke loose and dropped a short distance, broke apart and started a small avalanche of white and blue ice and brown rock.

The first sound would be a loud report, like a jet pushing through the sound barrier, followed by a heavy thump echoing from the middle of the mountain. We felt the pressure waves then heard the sound. The avalanches that followed hissed and roared like a waterfall. Fresh snow following a storm billowed up into a tear-shaped cloud. Without fresh snow it might not be possible to spot the avalanche before it stopped.

Halfway to Camp Muir the Nisqually Ice Fall completely dominates the view across the width of the mountain and upward for three to four thousand feet. All we could see were the ice falls and the massive outcropping of the iced eastern ridge of Gibraltar Rock on the right. The summit was somewhere beyond the view of the arching skyline, between the top of the blue shadowed ice falls and the rust colored basalt cliffs of the "Gib."

Gibraltar Rock looks like a slice of a many-layered chocolate cake. It was formed as one lava flow after another spewed out of the crater, piled up century after century and was then carved by the glaciers and rotted by the process of weathering. It is possible for huge sections of the "Gib" to break off and destroy anything in the path below it. Camp Muir is near the base of Gibraltar Rock.

Richard Rose had been guiding Judy from Paradise. He desperately wanted her to succeed. The night before, after the group meeting, he had gone to her room to express his sense of loss at her decision. He wanted to take something of hers to the summit. Now he was trying to show everybody that she could make it. She was carrying only a day

JULY 1, MT. RAINIER, DAY 3

pack and was doing well. After a rest stop and lunch he started out too fast and Judy started to weaken.

I took over for Rich and slowed down her pace. With Jim in front I didn't have to worry about the others getting lost on their way to Muir. I lapsed into my chant on breathing and resting until Judy regained a rhythm and breathing pattern which matched her energy level. Then for nearly two hours the only sounds were the repetitive crunch of heavy boots kicking into snow. My thoughts drifted back over many trips to Muir over the past thirty years of hiking, skiing, and climbing. When a person is in shape, the easy pace of a long climb on snow is perhaps one of the most peaceful of body experiences. The body relaxes and effort dissolves into the sound of wind and the warmth of the sun reflecting off the snow. The steady pace becomes somnambulistic. Thoughts are punctuated by even, deep, lung-filling breaths.

"Boom" The mountain spoke.
Inhale, "...there's an avalanche up there somewhere."
Exhale, "... above the Gib"
Inhale, "... Sounded like a big block of ice."
Exhale, "...I wonder where?"
Inhale, "... It's so far above me that by the time the sound gets here the ice blocks have stopped falling."
Exhale, "...Look some more, sometimes falling ice looks like a river or waterfall."
Inhale "...How is Judy doing? Turn around and look."
Exhale, "...Looks fine."

Inhale, "...I've always wondered how it sounded when the front end of Gibraltar rock"

Exhale, "... fell off in 1952. They closed the Gib route." Inhale, "...There's a spider on the snow."

Exhale, "...Blew up on a warm wind from the valley below."

Inhale,"...Glaciers and snow fields are covered with bugs." Exhale, "...Snow worms? --too early."

Inhale, "...Hmmm. Where's the bottle of snow worms I collected in 1957."

Exhale,"...Alaska. Lots of snow worms. Never did see a snow flea."

Inhale,"... They're supposed to exist in Greenland and Alaska."

"Phil. How much further?" Judy broke in.

Exhale. "Another twenty-five minutes. You're doing great, Judy. Did you hear that large avalanche a few minutes ago?"

"Yeh. Kind of scary. Is that the kind that killed the climbers last week?" Judy asked.

Exhale. "Probably, if they were under one that sounded like that."

Judy and I arrived at Camp Muir thirty to forty minutes behind the others. By taking a slow pace Judy arrived at Camp Muir relatively relaxed. We were all at Camp Muir just before sunset.

Everybody was tired but elated. Doug said it was the most demanding physical thing he had ever done in his life. He wondered if he could

JULY 1, MT. RAINIER, DAY 3

make the summit but decided he really wanted to. Jim explained that getting to Muir is the hardest part.

Camp Muir is the primary base camp for several routes up Rainier. There is a large kidney-bean-shaped, flat commons area outlined with large boulders. East of the commons area the snow field is flat. Climbers can pitch tents in the snow or they can stay in a public shelter on the south side of the commons.

The shelter is a stone building thirty feet long, fifteen feet wide and eight feet high. The only opening is the door. Inside there are bunks that will hold approximately twenty climbers, and a shelf to hold stoves. Melting snow had flooded the floor with an inch of water.

The Guide Service has a bunk shack on the northwest side of the commons, a rectangular fifteen-by-twenty-foot box, covered with tar paper and a tar roof that will sleep twenty to twenty-five. Bunks are three tiers high. The head room at the top level is so low it is impossible to sit up. The Guides also have a storage building and higher up on the rocks to the north, above the other building, a cookhouse. In addition to the four buildings, there are a couple of chemical toilets and a rack of refuse containers which are carried out by helicopter twice during the year.

On my first trip to Camp Muir in 1952, before the guide bunk shack and cook house, there was a traditional outhouse with a hole that opened over a cliff. The next year somebody forgot to close the door. Snow and ice filled the outhouse and it never thawed out.

PELION

The view back down the slope is to the south. In the clear air the distant peaks of Mt. Hood and the Three Sisters in Oregon stood as reference points for the height of volcanic peaks above the countryside. Mt. Adams (11,000 feet) and Mt. St. Helens (8,000 feet) appeared as giant neighbors above the waves of four-thousand-foot-high foothills.

A swath of destruction lay between St. Helens and Rainier. Steam clouds coming out of the dirty scar of Mt. St. Helens crater leaned out to the west in a gentle wind. A little more than a year before, St. Helens was 1,300 feet higher. It had erupted on May 18, 1980, leveling the forest and sending a shower of ash that covered eastern Washington. The snows of winter covered the ash that had fallen on the route to Muir.

Smoke from logging operations and slash burning filled several valleys. The ridges of the foothills lay in rows like a corduroy road toward the ocean. They blocked the low-angle sun, sending grey shadows into the smoke-filled valleys.

Stoves were placed on a large, fixed, outdoor table that stood about four feet high. Jim made dinner. Some ate standing up looking at the scenery; some ate sitting on the large chunks of volcanic basalt and pumice bordering the commons area.

We slid into our sleeping bags around ten o'clock. I slept in the Guide bunk shack with the disabled climbers. Our "porters" slept in the public shelter. The space was cramped on the sleeping platform-bunk and the blind sometimes had problems locating the opening to their sleeping bags.

JULY 1, MT. RAINIER, DAY 3

Justin inadvertently started to slide a leg into Bud's bag and stopped when Bud commented in a droll tone, "Queer." This caused a choking round of muffled laughter as we fell asleep. We tried to be quiet because another climbing party that was going directly to the summit had gone to bed around five in the afternoon and were already asleep. They would get up at midnight and climb all night while the snow was still solid and try to return before the late morning avalanches started.

The route up the mountain is on the eastern side and the snow starts getting soft and melting as soon as the sun rises. Pelion was planning only to go to high camp on the next day and would not have to get up until seven or eight. The only clue the early rising team might have to their unusual roommates was Charles' leg lying on the bench.

The summit party got up at midnight, climbed to the summit while we slept, and returned to Muir while the Pelion crew was gorging itself on pancakes. The guide reported that the route was in great shape.

CHAPTER 11

JULY 2, MT. RAINIER, DAY 4. HIGH CAMP

Judy was going to stay at Camp Muir until high camp was set up. She felt strong when getting to Muir and was disappointed that she had to remain behind. Joanne Lennox, one of the many volunteers who had generously donated two or three days stayed with Judy during the day and sorted out extra supplies. I had planned that some of the climbers would return from high camp for a second trip up with more supplies. I would then take Judy to high camp.

Ropes were required from Camp Muir to high camp. Jim led the first team of four. He traversed up to and across the top of the Cowlitz Glacier, moving from west to east in a long arc along the base of Gibraltar Rock, past Cadaver Gap, an ice fall, then past the base of Cathedral Rock, gaining one hundred vertical feet over a half-mile distance.

The rest of the teams followed Jim's path in single file. Breaking trail in the soft snow was tiring and it was easier to follow in the tracks of the team in front. The climbing party encountered the first of a number of small crevasses a couple hundred yards from Muir. Each blind climber came up to the edge of a crevasse and using a ski pole like a cane stuck the pole into the hole. They flicked it back and forth between the two sides to judge how far they would have to jump. Their belayer would pull the rope snug as the climber jumped. Occasionally they would misjudge a step and drop in up to their waist and then crawl out on the other side.

Shortly after leaving Muir we traversed under the steep ice fall coming down from Cadaver Gap which separated Gibraltar Rock and Cathedral Rock. High camp was just a little beyond the other side of Cadaver Gap but we traveled the long way around to get there. Warren Thompson of the Everest climbers mentioned that this is where Willie Unsoeld was killed in 1979. Unsoeld was from the Pacific Northwest and an internationally known climber. He and another climber had been descending from Cadaver Gap during a winter climb and were trapped in an avalanche that swept across the area we were now crossing.

The minutes passed as we began to traverse along the base of Cathedral Rock which is the steep barrier separating the Cowlitz Glacier, which we were on, and Ingraham Glacier on which we would camp. Already we could hear rocks melting loose from the weathered, red basalt, volcanic rock cliff rising 600 feet above us. The constant process of thawing during the day and freezing at night levers the weathered rock loose, dropping it onto the glacier below and leaving large piles of rock and rust-colored stains.

We were far enough below the cliff that we didn't have to worry about anything falling directly on us and didn't have to climb over the rocks. Rocks falling in the early morning or at night would land on

JULY 2, MT. RAINIER, DAY 4. HIGH CAMP

frozen slopes and slide further down the glacier onto our path. During the day those rocks would absorb heat from the sun and melt a hole in the snow. Over a period of a week or two the rocks would melt a hole eight to sixteen inches deep, depending on the size of the rock. Rocks larger than two feet in diameter did not absorb enough energy to melt their way into the surface. As the hole got deeper the rim of the hole cast a shadow over the rock. Eventually the rock would catch rays of the sun and get warm only at high noon and the hole wouldn't get any deeper unless it rained. As the glacier melted around the larger rocks a small pedestal could form. Over a period of time the rock would be raised above the surface of the glacier.

Water from rain would run off the rocks and melt the snow. The smaller rocks would roll into the water-made cavity. Rocks could wander from one place to another depending on the direction of the wind during a rain storm. Occasionally a climber would step on a sunken rock and the spikes of the crampons would grind on the hard surface. Sometimes a small rock jammed in between the spikes and had to be pried loose.

The traverse below Cathedral Rock ended at the opening to a very steep snow chute which led upward and was used to climb to the Ingraham Glacier. Getting into the opening required that we move across a rock fall area and around some large rock outcroppings.

The sun heating the rock mass had softened and melted the snow for several feet around. Climbing past the outcropping into the gully, we sank in up to our knees and hips. It was a difficult task even for those who could see where they were going to step. As we rounded the outcropping we coiled the rope so it would not tangle on the rocks. Then we could give a hand to the blind climbers. Once in the gully we let the full length of the rope out again.

The chute took us up three hundred vertical feet to the Ingraham Glacier. This was by far the steepest slope we had been on, and with heavy packs it was difficult for the blind team members to maintain their balance. Each step was made as a deliberate, planned effort. Voices reverberated off the walls on both sides. Justin could be heard talking to some distant galactic entity as a diversion. "Hello universe, come in, come in." He felt he was climbing into space.

Doug lost his balance and slid down a couple of times causing him to comment on the law against mountain climbing that Whittaker had mentioned - the law of gravity.

The top of the chute opened onto a dirty ridge of ground volcanic rock where we could look back to Camp Muir, as well as north onto the Ingraham Glacier and onto Little Tahoma, an 11,000-foot-peak on the eastern side of Rainier. The original Indian name for Rainier is Tahoma. There was Big Tahoma and Little Tahoma. We had reached a logical place to rest.

For twenty minutes we munched on Gorp, drank juice, put on more sun cream and generally enjoyed ourselves. There was a nice echo off the southern end of Cathedral Rock and I went over to find a good

JULY 2, MT. RAINIER, DAY 4. HIGH CAMP

place to practice yodeling. I thought it was the most fantastic echo I had ever heard. I yodeled again. I was feeling pretty good about my yodeling and turned around to see everyone rolling around holding their sides laughing. Unknown to me Doug was making a recording and when I stopped yodeling he was playing it back.

After the break Jim led off again and took the team along the north side of Cathedral Rock heading in the direction of the summit. The trail curved up and to the right over a snow bridge and onto the Ingraham Glacier. From there the slope was gentle for about a half-mile before gradually getting steeper, transforming into a cascading, slow-motion waterfall called the Ingraham Ice Falls - a jumble of crevasses and shredded snow bridges. Jim traversed to the right under the ice falls and onto a small, relatively flat spot appropriately called the Ingraham Flats. He indicated this was where high camp was to be set up.

Facing uphill, Cadaver Gap is on the left. The Gap is a narrow pass between Cathedral Rocks and the lower eastern flank of Gibraltar Rock. Two hundred yards to the right was Disappointment Cleaver, a large shoulder of a ridge that separated the Ingraham and Emmons glaciers. The large ice fall, the area where the eleven climbers were still buried from the avalanche eleven days before, was between high camp and the Cleaver.

When Jim reached high camp, the last person was still a quarter of a mile behind. Climbing ropes are 160 feet long. When five or six ropes are stretched out and there is a distance of fifty to sixty feet between ropes, there is a total distance of 1,100 to 1,200 feet between the lead climber and the last person.

When I reached high camp I dropped my big pack, took a small day pack, and was ready to go down for another load of supplies and Judy. Bud Krogh and Joe Wishcamper, two lawyers turned Sherpa to help carry gear to high camp, headed back to Camp Muir with me.

Four members of the 1984 Everest climbing team who were serving as porters planned to follow. We moved rapidly down the Ingraham Glacier to the top of the steep chute that dropped down onto the Cowlitz that we had climbed earlier. Near the bottom of the chute we passed Steve Marts and two guides who were climbing to high camp. Steve had climbed a number of the world's most difficult mountains as a cameraman. I could never figure out how he got to the top to photograph the first climber ever to reach the summit. He was going up to join Ridgeway and the film crew as a second cameraman. We chatted briefly. I had met Steve while still planning Pelion.

Judy and Joanne were ready when we arrived at Camp Muir. Bud Krogh continued on down to Paradise to return to Seattle to attend a wedding. Earlier I had invited Bud to go to the summit with us. We had done a number of things together as kids. We used to rappel out the third floor window at his home until his mother objected to the footprints on the wall. Years later he was on the staff at the White House under Nixon and had had his public service career interrupted by the avalanche of issues in the Watergate and Ellsberg cases. Now he was carrying heavy loads for a group of handicapped climbers.

JULY 2, MT. RAINIER, DAY 4. HIGH CAMP

Joe and I loaded up packs with food and lanterns. Joanne set out the rest of the equipment for the Everest team to take up. Joanne's husband, Monte had gone to high camp and returned before we had. He was already packed to head back up.

When Judy was ready I tied her in the middle of the rope and put Joe Wishcamper on the end. The Everest climbers arrived just as we were leaving Camp Muir. Joanne and Monte and the Everest team caught up and passed us, upward bound along the base of Cathedral Rocks just before the steep snow chute. As we approached the opening to the chute the clatter of loose rocks was more frequent. Under the afternoon sun melting snow was now trickling down, forming a small stream next to the outcropping. We filled our water bottles and took a sip before starting up the forty-five degree and steeper snow chute. By now the snow had softened the steep slope and it was easy to kick an evenly spaced sequence of steps for Judy to follow.

Judy, Joe and I plodded on with an easy rhythm, using the rest step and arrived at high camp only twenty minutes behind the Everest team. Judy had made it to high camp, non-stop, in two and one-half hours. The rest of the team had eaten and were already sleeping. Though she said she felt good, she was so tired she couldn't hold a cup of soup in her hands.

High camp consisted of eleven tents bound on the south and north sides by crevasses, a steep slope rising above us to the summit on the west, and a panoramic view to the east looking over the top of Little Tahoma. Glaciers flowed past Little Tahoma on both sides and disappeared into the valleys and forests that stretched into eastern Washington. East of Rainier the foothills get progressively smaller, and eventually the countryside flattens out into an orange haze of wheat fields. In the distance the windshield of a car flashed a burst of reflected sunlight. The shiny roof of a barn stood like a beacon in the midst of a sea of flat country.

First arrivals at high camp had dug a platform out of the slope for each tent. Thirty feet above the tents and to the left was the "bathroom," which consisted of a hole dug in the snow with a place on either side for positioning feet. Use of the facility was an acrobatic, public activity. A rope to the left of the "bathroom" warned there was a crevasse on the other side.

An outdoor kitchen had been made by digging a platform six feet wide and three feet deep. A shelf to hold the stove and extra food was carved out of the snow. Snow was melted for water for dinner, coffee, tea, hot chocolate, and to fill the drinking bottles.

Jim and I encouraged everybody to get to sleep. Climbing would start early. Jim said he would wake everybody up at two. Climbers had prepared their smaller climbing packs and crawled into their tents. Except for Doug, Kirk and Justin who could be heard quietly talking about the dead climbers and that they would have to walk where the dead were buried, there were no other conversations. Everybody was tired from the day's climb and the altitude. Jim stretched out ropes so all we had to do was tie in and we could get started quickly.

JULY 2, MT. RAINIER, DAY 4. HIGH CAMP

Jim, Dianne and I assigned climbers to rope teams, balancing the strength of the guides with the strengths of the different climbers. We wrote out the names of each team and cross-checked to make sure everybody was included. When we were finished, I crawled into the opening of my tent and turned around and sat with my feet sticking out. Judy and Svein Gilje, one of the two reporters climbing with us, were already asleep. I took off my boots and banged them together to knock the snow off, then zipped up the tent. I used the boots and a sweater for a pillow.

It was quiet outside except for the rustling of a plastic garbage bag in the kitchen area as a gentle breeze came down the glacier from the summit. Periodically a few rocks would fall down the face of Cathedral Rocks and drop into the open space of a schrund, the deep gap formed by the glacier pulling away from the cliff. Even the sound seemed locked into the ice.

Even though there are acres of snow and ice, the space available for a camp site is limited. The eleven tents were on both sides of the trail up the mountain. Around midnight a ranger and climbing party passed through camp. I could hear the slow, steady crunch of crampons biting into ice, their rope sliding over the frozen snow crystals, and the ring of the metal ice axes being stabbed into the frozen snow as they were used as walking staffs. They were on their way to the summit in search of a person who had been wandering on the summit for a week on a religious quest. An hour later another climbing party traveled through.

PELION

ROPE TEAMS

Rope 1: Jim Whittaker
Alec Naiman (Deaf)
Kirk Adams (Blind)
Chuck O'Brien (Amputee)

Rope 2: Roy Fitzgerald
Tim Egan - Reporter
Sheila Holzworth (Blind)
Dianne Roberts

Rope 3: Nancy Goforth (Volunteer Ranger)
Fred Noesner Blind)
George Neibel (Everest)
Justin McDevitt (Blind)

Rope 4: Phil Bartow
Bud Keith (Blind)
Svein Gilje (Reporter)
Paul Stefurak (Deaf)

Rope 5: Warren Thompson (Everest)
Doug Wakefield (Blind)
Richard Rose (Epileptic)
Ray Nichols (Everest)

CHAPTER 12

JULY 3, MT. RAINIER, DAY 5, THE SUMMIT

Jim woke camp at two, lit the stoves and started to melt snow and heat water for instant oatmeal and coffee. Though below freezing, the night air felt warm and held promise of a hot day. We would leave down-filled pants in the tents. At two in the morning there is fuzziness in sounds and voices.

Fitz was in the tent with Bud and Doug. He tried to dress in the dark, confined space and had to turn on his light. For a while he stopped and watched Bud and Doug methodically dressing...pants, boots, sweaters, parka...in their own form of darkness.

There was a continuous rustle of sleeping bags and parkas brushing against the sides of tents and the muffled banging of cups and spoons as climbers crawled out of their domed tents onto the ice. Their boots crunched and squeaked on the snow. Communications seemed limited to grunting acknowledgments. By three-thirty everybody was struggling to put on crampons.

Jim was yelling, "Come on gang, let's get this show on the road." He knew that even though everybody was excited about the climb, at three in the morning it is easy to go back to sleep and dream about getting ready.

Finally each person was tied in to a rope and moving before the early rays of morning light stabbed over the tops of the mountains and the thin clouds on the horizon to the east. The trail moved out of camp and down a small ramp onto the jumbled path of the ice fall. The teams stretched the ropes as they moved down the avalanche track, around ice blocks the size of cars, toward the base of Disappointment Cleaver, the rock buttress separating the Ingraham and the Emmons Glaciers.

Doug asked Warren Thompson, one of the Everest team, about the climbers who had died as he moved across the broken surface, "Is this where they were camped?"

"No," Warren said, "They weren't camped. They were just climbing by."

Doug sensed a void on his right. "What's that down there?"

"A big crevasse."

The full realization of the tragedy set in. "Is that the crevasse they were swept into?"

JULY 3, MT. RAINIER, DAY 5, THE SUMMIT

"Yes." Warren responded in a monotone.

Doug felt a surge of energy. "Let's get the hell out of here!" His team moved across the avalanche path about the time the sun's rays bathed the eastern slopes of the mountain in brilliant pink, creating deep blue shadows. The pink mountain was etched in the black night sky with brilliant stars to the west. At these altitudes there is little dust in the air to diffuse the light; and pink snow, blue shadows and the night sky accentuate each other. The light was now bright enough for the film crew to take pictures.

Jim had put in fixed lines across the face of the Cleaver the day before. They were anchored to the rock face every fifty to sixty feet and served as a railing. At first the trail was a six-inch ledge scuffed out of the top of the snow where it joined the vertical rock.

Bud was hesitantly moving across the face of the Cleaver. At times he would get a step or two off the track before I could turn around and redirect him, and remind Svein to pay more attention to Bud. I was trying to keep my eye on Justin, who was last on the third rope.

Doug questioned Warren, "Is this the most dangerous part?"

"Yes."

"From rock fall?"

"Yes."

"If something comes down, what do I do… duck?"

"Press in against the wall."

Doug's perception of the shape of the mountain was becoming more vivid.

The red volcanic rock cliff seemed to be held together by the ice. During the warmth of the day pieces would melt loose and drop from above onto the steep slope and bounce into the chasm below.

The route moved around the buttress and opened onto a steep snow slope that dropped off to the right into a huge crevasse. The path, the width of a climbing boot, moved diagonally up and across the slope for a hundred yards. It then turned left and headed straight up a fifty-degree slope for three hundred feet to the first of a series of rock outcroppings following the backbone of the Cleaver. The blind climbers had to scrape each foot along the left edge of the path to make sure they didn't step off the right side.

I climbed past the face of the Cleaver and was inching my way onto the steep slope for the traverse. Justin was in front of me. Fred, in second position on the rope with Justin, couldn't set his crampon properly. He lost his balance slipped off the narrow path and started to fall. He was grasping for his ice axe and struggling to attain the self-arrest position. I stopped breathing as Fred fell. He dropped fifteen feet before his

JULY 3, MT. RAINIER, DAY 5, THE SUMMIT

self-arrest and belayer stopped him. The practice in Colorado and on the Nisqually had paid off.

Climbing up the Cleaver involved moving up a series of small rock outcroppings. We would climb from one, then up the steep snow slope several hundred feet to another outcrop. A sighted climber would arrive at the outcropping and pull in the rope. Tim could be heard talking to Sheila.

"Move a little left … There's a good place for your foot on the right of the rock in front of you …The ice is rotten in front of you. It might break through but doesn't go anywhere so don't worry."

…"Fantastic move. You're doing great, Sheila."

A brief rest was usually taken at the outcroppings. During one rest stop Doug said, "I hear a jet, a big one. It sounds like it is down there." He pointed north of Little Tahoma.

I suggested it was a jumbo jet heading for SEA-TAC airport and it was over a thousand feet below us.

"I guess we are pretty high up," he commented.

Climbers separated by the length of the rope had a chance to see how each was doing, nibble some Gorp and drink juice. Rich mentioned to me on one rest stop that he'd had a seizure. We discussed it, and Rich felt it wasn't affecting his strength, balance or judgment.

On the third outcropping the second and third ropes were resting. Jim had already led the first team higher up and his moose call was echoing off Gibraltar Rock. I was one hundred feet below and the fifth team was below mine. My Handi-Talkie started squawking and I turned it up. "Special Message." This was a pre-arranged signal. I yelled up to Steve Marts, a cameraman, to focus on Chuck; then called to Chuck to turn on his radio.

"...Twins...," was the message. Chuck O'Brien had become the father of twins, a boy and a girl. With a few shouts of joy and congratulations Chuck's team continued up the slope. The twins were later named Matthew James Rainier, after Jim; and Meagan Elizabeth Tahoma.

The route from about 12,200 feet to the summit moved from the Ingraham to the Emmons glacier and switched back and forth up a relatively smooth but steep snow slope. A small depression on the slope at 12,800 feet was used for a rest stop. Team four arrived as team two was leaving.

I noticed that Bud Keith was having trouble. He had been pulling on the rope all morning for support. He wasn't getting enough oxygen. He had been reminded several times to breathe harder but hadn't been able to make the adjustments. Now he was beginning to shake violently and had started to vomit; the symptoms of altitude sickness. We decided it was best to leave Bud with Ray Nichols, one of the Everest climbers on Pelion's team five, who agreed to stay with Bud. Warren Thompson, lead climber on team five, was carrying a sleeping bag and pad. A recessed platform was dug for Bud and Ray. Bud

JULY 3, MT. RAINIER, DAY 5, THE SUMMIT

gave me the bag of jelly beans he was carrying to the top for President Reagan, and the International Year of Disabled Persons (IYDP) flag.

Once Bud and Ray were secure we continued up the slope, followed by Warren's team, to rendezvous with the others at 13,800 feet. It was now 7:30 AM. We had been climbing for four hours from high camp. The climbing was rhythmic. Step, rest, breathe, step, rest, breathe. There were no obstacles, it was warm, and the pace was comfortable, relaxing and peaceful.

This was the first time in two weeks that it was quiet and I didn't have to be planning. I only had to put one foot in front of the other. My thoughts wandered over the many events of the past two weeks. I felt that a lifetime of climbing experience was coming into focus in a sharing with a team that might not otherwise have had the chance.

How are the others doing? I wondered. They seem strong, enthusiastic and excited. Chuck must be in a certain amount of pain. The blisters on his stump looked pretty sore. Fitz had been helping Chuck with dressing the blisters throughout the trip. Chuck could probably measure every step with a twinge of pain.

Several of the blind climbers had expressed their uncertainty associated with each step while crossing the steep face of the Cleaver below us. The simplicity and forcefulness of the climbing experience as a statement of how people deal with pain and uncertainty caught up with me. We have a summit, an objective and a belief in what we are doing. Given a meaningful objective, people will find a way to deal with the pain and uncertainty. They have been doing it all week. If we can do anything for others it is to help them identify meaningful objectives for themselves.

A helicopter droning up the valley broke into my thoughts. "Damn, that noise will foul up the film team's recordings."

Near 13,800 feet we passed the climbing group that had gone through camp before we got up. They were dead tired, sitting in the snow and staring blankly as we climbed past them step by step. The "disabled" climbers of Pelion were moving well; they were strong, had been well prepared and were doing everything right.

Jim stopped a little higher up for a break and indicated the summit was not very far away. In fact, while Warren and I were still at 13,800 feet, we could hear Jim, as lead on the first rope, shouting back that he could see the crater rocks. At 10:40 Jim's team reached the rocks of the south rim of the crater, and Kirk Adams became the first blind person to reach the top of Rainier. Every five to ten minutes another team would arrive to an increasing crescendo of shouts and cheers. The sound carries well, and even though some were on top, the climbing seemed to go on and on and on. Finally, all the teams were on the rim.

The group was jubilant.

Jim played the bard on the summit leading a chorus.
Jim: "If there is an ocean." Chorus: "We cross it."
Jim: "When there is a disease." Chorus: "We cure it."

JULY 3, MT. RAINIER, DAY 5, THE SUMMIT

Jim: "When there is a record." Chorus: "We break it."
Jim: "When there is a wrong." Chorus: "We right it."
Jim: "When there is a mountain." Chorus: "We climb it."

It was a historic moment not only in mountaineering, but for each person. No blind person had ever climbed the mountain before. We had a team of five who were blind, an amputee, two who were deaf and a person with epilepsy on top.

I contacted the Motorola communications center at Paradise and reported that Pelion was on the summit. Rich Rose shouted, "Here's one for the epileptics!"

Tim and Svein, from competing newspapers, were trying to make contact on their radios with their counterparts at Paradise to report the event. Svein was hoping he could make the evening edition deadline. Tim's paper would report the story in the morning. Planes were flying overhead, obviously taking pictures. A Seattle TV film crew and Ridgeway documentation crew were cranking away on film. Dianne was taking pictures for Pelion on one camera and for different media groups on other cameras.

Flags were flown in the gentle breeze: The US flag, the IYDP flag for the United Nations, and the Washington State flag.

I unwrapped the four eagle feathers and placed the shaft on which they were mounted in the snow in front of the team. The feathers danced and spun around, the colored beads flashing in the sunlight. I opened the medicine bundle while explaining my instructions from Joe Washington. A pinch of the medicine was offered to the east, then a pinch to the south, a pinch to the west, a pinch to the north, a pinch to heaven and a pinch to the earth. The remainder of the bundle would be offered to a fire after the team returned to the base of the mountain.

The night before the climb to Camp Muir Judy had given Rich Rose her St. Christopher's medal. On the rim of the summit he raised it above his head and spoke about how he felt about the team and Judy's presence in thought and spirit.

Dianne handed out some Tofflers Chocolate, and Charles opened a beer and passed it around. Every few minutes somebody would whoop or holler with a spontaneous burst of enthusiasm and everybody joined in.

We planned to cross the crater to sign the summit register. To avoid the question of who got there first, I had everybody march hand-in-hand across the crater to the register. Snow and ice fill the inside of the crater, forming a large field a half-mile across. The rim rises fifteen to fifty feet above the floor. Steam vents around the edges both melt the snow and provide the moisture for irregular ice formations on the barren, pumice-strewn crater rim. The colors were intense: a brilliant blue sky, white snow, and reddish-brown rim rock. The air in the crater bowl was still and warm.

The register, a bound notebook, is kept in a metal box fifteen by eight by three inches. Another group was signing their names when

JULY 3, MT. RAINIER, DAY 5, THE SUMMIT

the Pelion team arrived. After a cordial exchange, they handed over the register.

I wrote a description of Project Pelion, then the register was passed around so each person could sign it. The register read:

"PROJECT PELION (symbolizing opportunity and access for all.) Project Pelion is a climb of Mt. Rainier by a team of disabled persons in recognition of the International Year of Disabled Persons."

Jim expressed concern about the lateness of the day. It would have been nice to bask in the sun on the summit, but dangers increase with the heat of the afternoon. Sun-warmed snow causes avalanches. Rocks frozen in the ice melt loose. The firm morning snow softens and climbers can sink up to their waists in an exhausting struggle. Soft snow clings to crampons, filling the spikes with a heavy, clumsy ball of packed snow rendering the crampons ineffective and causing the feet to slip.

The later it is in the day, the more difficult and dangerous the descent becomes. It was twelve-thirty before the teams were roped up and starting down. The communication center was notified. They asked when the team would arrive at the lodge. Jim asked to have milkshakes and hamburgers ready at 1:30 the next day.

Fred had worn a red, white and blue scarf around his neck from the first day in Colorado. Fred had lost his sight to cancer at the age of four. His first daughter, whose scarf he was wearing, had died of the same disease at the age of four. He had worn the scarf as a memorial to her. As he started off the south rim for the descent he stopped, stood for a moment and then shoved a bamboo trail wand into the snow. Slowly he untied the scarf from around his neck, kissed it and secured it to the wand. He cradled it in both hands, then gently ran one hand over it like a loving father stroking the head of his child and slowly walked away. The scarf, highlighted by an endless expanse of blue sky, waved in the soft breeze.

On the upward climb the slope is only a few inches in front of the climber, providing a feeling of security. On the descent, the slope falls away and the bottom of the valleys are thousands of feet below. The crampons were clogging with snow, forcing some climbers to stop every two or three steps and hit the sides of their feet with their ice axes to knock the snow loose.

Some developed a rhythm for hitting a foot every time they took a step. Others slipped, twisted their ankles and struggled to stay balanced on every third or fourth step. A sense of urgency set in. New muscles were being used and tired muscles were more apparent. Climbing down seemed more exhausting than climbing up.

Dianne and I stopped our teams when we arrived at the platform where Bud and Ray Nichols had spent the day. Bud had recovered from his altitude sickness but was overwhelmed by a sense of sadness. He felt bad about not making the summit. He felt he had let down a lot of people. Dianne sat with him and let him know that no honor was lost. He had done more than many do, had climbed higher than many sighted do; and that Pelion had succeeded and he was a part of Pelion.

JULY 3, MT. RAINIER, DAY 5, THE SUMMIT

Football-sized chunks of snow were cascading down from the team above. Ray Nichols saw a large piece falling toward Bud, jumped to protect him, and stepped on Bud's water bottle with his crampons. Bud said, "That's OK; I stepped on another one this morning."

Bud was tied onto the rope in front of me and behind Paul Stefurak. We continued down, descended five hundred feet, and moved to a flat spot above the rock ridges. The first few steps off the rocky ledges into the snow were the most difficult. As the afternoon had progressed, the sun warmed and softened the surface so that every few steps a person would break through and fall into a hole up to their hips, or the crampons would become clogged with snow causing the climber to slip.

Paul Stefurak hesitated and wanted to rest. He took his pack off. I motioned for him to keep moving. Every minute was adding to the instability of the slope, and he was putting his and other lives at risk. He was adamant, didn't want to communicate, and refused to read a note I wrote. He insisted that I sign to him. When I made a mistake, he would laugh. I gave him a couple of signs he understood.

I threw his pack down the steep slope we had to descend and signed with a closed fist suggesting that he might be next. We climbed down to his pack. He again refused to continue the descent.

"For Christ's sake let's get moving. Do something," Bud said. He was getting nervous about getting off the mountain. "We can't play games all the way down." Even with Svein on the rope, who had expressed some concern but was being quiet, we didn't have the strength to drag

Paul and not make Bud's condition worse. My concerns in Colorado were being realized. We were in a dangerous setting and Paul was acting out a life of frustration.

Warren Thompson and Ray Nickols, two of the Everest climbers, were on the rope behind us with Rich Rose. As they started to move by I untied Paul, gesturing I would leave him. He played along calling my bluff. He knew that I would not leave him, but he couldn't hear me telling Warren and Ray to get ready to tie Paul onto their rope. They were strong enough and could drag him down if necessary. As they started past, Rich Rose quickly untied from their rope, and I distracted Paul long enough to get him clipped with a carabineer onto the rope Rich had vacated with a carabineer. Warren and Ray wasted no time in muscling Paul down the slope. I put Rich Rose at the front of my rope.

Rich had been a person I could turn to when somebody needed help. He was patient, level-headed and compassionate. When Judy had needed moral support and a guide, Rich had been there to help her. As soon as Rich was clipped in, we headed down the seven hundred feet to the top of the Cleaver. From there the camp was visible a thousand feet below to the right. Jim's team could be seen already working its way through the avalanche track into camp.

In camp Judy and Joe Wishcamper had spent the day lounging around. In the morning Judy had planned to sleep through the departure of the team, but there was too much excitement. Then she thought she would go to sleep after the team left, but found she could follow

JULY 3, MT. RAINIER, DAY 5, THE SUMMIT

their progress by the sound of their voices around the Cleaver. Once the climbers moved around the buttress, it grew quiet but as they moved up above the Cleaver their voices carried down a thousand to fifteen hundred feet. Later in the day as the climbers were descending their voices could again be heard above the Cleaver. The sounds would be quieted by the buttress and then would boom out as the climbers came around the bottom of the cliff.

Bud was getting apprehensive about the traverse down across the face of the Cleaver. It had worried him all day. While climbing up he kept asking, "How do we get down this? How do we get down this?" and now he was further distracted by the confrontation with Paul. I called Jim on the Handi-Talkie and asked if he would climb up to the top of the traverse and take Bud. By the time Rich Rose got down to the edge of the Cleaver, Jim and Rick Ridgeway were already arriving after a fast climb up from camp. They tied Bud in between them and then headed down, disappearing over the line of snow and blue sky. I belayed Rich who followed Jim.

When climbing up a slope the experienced climber goes first to find the route and to hold the people who follow, should they fall. When descending, the experienced climber goes last in order to hold the people in front, should they fall.

Moving off the slope above the Cleaver head wall onto the steep face is like walking off a roof onto a very high ladder. Suddenly there is nothing in front of you except a void and a very narrow trough wide enough for only one foot. It is necessary to squat to be able to move a foot down. Moving down and to the right required the right foot to be moved between the left leg and the wall of snow without snagging a crampon on the left pant leg. There was a sense that a slip here would result in a long fall, and a slip was all too likely.

Both the blind and sighted moved cautiously, making sure that they first knocked the snow out of their crampons and that each foot was securely placed in the middle of the small trough that was forming by the passage of climbers. It is difficult to plant the downhill foot firmly when squatting; so you put your foot down and transfer weight to it hoping the crampon will dig into the surface. Each step was calculated, deliberate, and acknowledged with a sigh of relief.

Rocks falling off the Cleaver and sliding over the trail during the afternoon made small tracks which ended at the edge of the precipice below. Several large tracks cutting across the trail suggested that some of the rocks that had fallen during the afternoon were big enough to knock a whole rope team off the steep slope of the Cleaver face.

As we progressed slowly across the face, Rick, Bud and Jim were out of my sight around the corner of the Cleaver buttress. Rich Rose, first on my rope, was also out of sight, and Svein, in front of me, was rounding the corner. I could see the tents below and Nancy, Fred, George and Justin in team three crossing the avalanche track between the Cleaver and camp.

CHAPTER 13

JULY 3, MT. RAINIER, DAY 5 AVALANCHE

The initial grinding sound of an avalanche of ice falling and the cries to run took time to reach me. I could already see climbers trying to run. Fred and Justin were unable to follow the twisting path and were running in different directions. They were jerked off their feet by the rope.

When they got up and tried to run again they fell. This was the exact spot where the people were sitting when they were killed the week before. Fred and Justin were disoriented and ran into ice blocks left from the devastating avalanche from the previous week and fell. Their ropes tangled. When they tried to get up they were again pulled off their feet or tripped. Nancy Goforth, the leader on their rope, was pulled off her feet, and when she tried to get up was pulled down again. The team disappeared from the view of those in camp.

Climbers already in their tents and some of the support team in high camp started to move from the tents and away from the roaring, crashing sound of the falling ice. Everybody was yelling, "Run!" or just screaming anything that would come out of their throats, panicked at the realization that the events of the week before were, against all reason, repeating themselves.

I was afraid that somebody would fall on their ice axe or step on another person with the two-inch crampon spikes. Bud, on Jim's rope, said he heard the ice crack and fall and felt the ground shake. "It sounded like a train."

Jim could see the block shear off from the towering jumble of ice near the top of the Cleaver and watched it fall. It hit an outcropping of rock and exploded into several parts, expanding the path of destruction. He sensed, based on a lifetime of guiding and climbing, that the block would break apart and that each of the smaller blocks would continue to fragment until none had the momentum to continue down the mountain onto the panicked climbers. The mass of ice twelve days before had been larger and had swept down the same slope another hundred feet to bury the eleven climbers.

Jim yelled, "It's OK; it's OK; it's OK!"

The last chunk of ice rolled within twenty feet of the climbers as they got to their feet. It took a few seconds to catch their breath and feel to see if any injuries had occurred. Jim reached them and headed up the last forty feet of slope to the tents. From where I was standing further up on the slope it looked as if Jim had picked Bud up by the pants and carried him across the avalanche track in a dead run. Bud later told me he had a surge of energy and told Rick Ridgeway to "stay ahead of me if you don't want to get run over."

JULY 3, MT. RAINIER, DAY 5 AVALANCHE

Fred Noesner, who was on a rope team that was directly under the fall and was miraculously spared, told me later that after he heard the sounds of the falling rock and ice slow and come to a stop he knew he was safe. He said the air tasted wonderful, the ground under his feet felt great. Every sound was vivid and pleasant.

As he walked back into camp with his heart still racing, he wanted to talk and share his joy with his fellow climbers. Hearing Kirk and Sheila talking quietly in a nearby tent, he moved to the open flap and greeted them. Understandably he was at first puzzled when Sheila screamed and started crying. He inquired what could be wrong on such a wonderful day. Between sobs, Sheila said, "You are dead!"

Kirk Explained. "They told us your rope team was buried in the ice fall." In the confusion and emotion of the moment, sighted climbers didn't relay the good news to the blind climbers in camp that the rope team in front of the avalanche had been spared. Fred assured Sheila that he was not a ghost.

A large rock swept across the slope in front of me as Rich Rose approached the avalanche track. Rich waited until Svein and I were off the traverse, then moved across the avalanche slope at a pace which did not reveal the exhaustion of fourteen hours of climbing and four minor epileptic seizures.

Warren's team came off the traverse last. They removed the fixed rope and the anchors as they moved down the face. There was a release of tension as they arrived.

The shock of the moments before set in on Justin. He was standing staring through unseeing eyes. I happened to be watching him as his fingers started to quiver, then shake, and then his whole body shook and tears poured down his face. I went over and hugged him and held him up. Several others came over to see if he was OK. He relaxed and we all congratulated one another.

Steve Marts unveiled a bottle of champagne. The bottle was passed around and everybody shared a toast to their unique accomplishment and narrow escape.

Climbing Mount Rainier is tiring. Most of the party went into their tents for a short nap before dinner and retiring for the night. Fitz checked with every person to see if any injuries had occurred during the ice fall. Everyone had escaped the ordeal without injury.

I mentioned to Fitz that Rich had had a couple of seizures going up. Fitz talked with him and discussed the four seizures Rich had had during the day and suggested an increase in the dosage of anticonvulsants. Rich had not had a seizure for three months prior to the climb.

CHAPTER 14

JULY 4, INDEPENDENCE DAY, PARADISE LODGE

During the night some of the climber's sleep was disturbed by the clattering of small avalanches and rock fall in the ice falls above camp and on the cleaver to the north. Just before sunrise most everyone was awakened by a roaring wind which traveled down the mountain. At first the tents were buffeted about and then were flattened by a blast of wind that pushed the tops of the dome tents onto the chests of those inside like a giant hand.

The wind quieted a little. Since it was too early to get up, most went back to sleep. At 6:30 I got up and put pots of snow on the stoves for water for coffee and instant breakfast. The wind continued thrashing the tents, and blew loose items lying around camp down into a crevasse. When anybody got out of their tent to pack, they had to hang onto unsecured items. Taking the tents down was a challenge. It took two to three people to hold down a tent and pack it after they removed the heavy packs and sleeping bags and crawled out.

PELION

The empty tents caught the wind and filled up like giant balloons. A pattern of lenticular, high wind clouds, which looked like a squadron of flying saucers, stretched to the east. A huge stationary, multi-layered cloud hung in a fixed position to the side of the summit. Typically these are the omens of a change in the weather. Since it had been nothing but fantastic, the change must be for the worse.

Joe Washington had given me the medicine staff with four eagle feathers. We'd had four perfect days of weather. It seemed like the same hand that stopped the ice fall before engulfing the teams in its path had pressed on the tents as a farewell gesture.

Two days before, a number of porters had helped carry tents and food up to high camp and then returned to Paradise. Much of the food had been eaten but the containers remained. Jim and I piled extra equipment, food and garbage bags onto our packs, pushing the weight to well over one-hundred and twenty pounds. The extra food would be carried down to Camp Muir and given to the guides.

Five people were tied to each rope for the descent to Camp Muir. The trench-like path and foot holes made during the heat of the previous day had frozen during the night. Early morning stiffness and the irregularity of the downhill trail made travel difficult for the blind climbers. With each step the weight of the body and the bulky pack drops down heavily on the forward leg, straining muscles and giving rise to a climbing malady called "downhill knee."

JULY 4, INDEPENDENCE DAY, PARADISE LODGE

There are few exercises to prepare for going down a mountain. Justin and Judy were having problems with their footing. They would slip every few steps and lose their balance or fall and have to struggle to their feet under the weight of their packs. It was exhausting.

By the time the team traversed the northern side of Cathedral Rocks above the Ingraham and prepared to descend the steep snow slope to Cowlitz Glacier, the snow was softening and would slide out from under our feet, adding to the general difficulty. The team did not bother to pause at the top of the ridge but plunged, climbed and slipped down the steep slope. The descent was certainly faster and easier than the climb up. From the bottom of the chute they traversed to the right across the top of the Cowlitz in a long semi-circular path to Camp Muir. Even though it had been only a couple of days since passing over the Cowlitz on the climb up, the crevasses were noticeably larger and many of the small snow bridges had melted or been collapsed under the feet of other climbers.

At Camp Muir the ropes were taken off, coiled and tied to the packs. They would not be needed again. The extra food was given to the cook in the guide's cookhouse, and the garbage was left in general refuse containers. Some miscellaneous items were recouped from the storage shed, and the team headed for Paradise Lodge.

Ski poles were used by the blind for stability. For the first mile below Muir the footing was awkward even for the sighted. Dozens of people had been to Muir the previous day and it was impossible to find an even sequence of steps in the still-frozen surface. With the growing excitement to get down we were trying to move faster than the conditions allowed. On every other step a foot would slip into a deep frozen foot hole and the weight of the pack would be thrown off balance. Though there was no danger of falling and sliding down a steep slope as there had been above, the going was very tiring. Doug found that walking independently and away from the beaten path was easier, almost as he imagined skiing would be.

As we descended to a lower altitude and time passed, the snow warmed and softened enough to let us make our own foot steps and the walking became easier. About a mile-and-a-half down Judy found she could move with an unusually easy pace by shuffling her feet over the surface like a cross-country skier. The pace picked up.

Jim, Dianne, Rich, Judy and I were in the rear. The question came up as to where people should regroup. While Pebble Creek, two miles above the lodge had been discussed, some uncertainty was expressed. Jim decided to catch up to talk to those in front. He stretched his long legs in a huge stride and disappeared down the slope.

Above Pebble Creek there is a series of steep inclines which are most easily descended in a sitting glissade. I checked each of the slopes for Judy to make sure there were no rocks at the base. She could then sit down and push off, drop twenty to thirty feet, and slide out across the flat bottom below.

JULY 4, INDEPENDENCE DAY, PARADISE LODGE

Friends of the Whittakers and others had carried sodas and beer up to Pebble Creek as a welcoming party. Everybody enjoyed getting out from under their packs. Kirk said he liked the feeling of floating that he had after he took off his pack. Dee Molenaar had hiked up and said he would have to add a new chapter to his classic book, THE CHALLENGE OF RAINIER.

There was a growing sense of excitement. We were almost off the mountain. Jim suggested that I take the lead down from Pebble Creek. The trail alternates between rock and dirt paths and snow. For the first quarter mile there were a few hikers sitting along the trail offering congratulations. There was a final steep section, then a mile-and-a-half of trail to Paradise Lodge.

At the top of the steep section several hundred people could be seen lining the trail below. Friends, relatives, the curious, other handicapped onlookers, reporters, camera crews, well wishers; all had hiked up to meet the team. Some had arrived before sunrise; some had driven from Florida and waited two days. The Motorola crew and Sheila's mother brought up a bottle of champagne. We stopped, drank the champagne, visited with friends and said hello to the television crews. From where we stood we could look down onto the Nisqually Glacier to where we had practiced in the crevasses, and look up the towering ice falls.

A reporter asked Fitz if he would identify which climbers had which handicap. Fitz replied that he couldn't remember, "They had become such complete people to me that I stopped identifying them as blind or deaf."

PELION

There was a hero's welcome all the way to the Visitor's Center. In a way it was a mob scene and Jim suggested that we just keep moving as fast as we could. The Pelion team arrived in front of the Center at 1:35 PM. Dusty, Judy's Seeing Eye dog was excited at her return. Paul's mother hung a wreath of flowers around his neck. The U.N. flag was held out to remind the crowd of the purpose of the climb. After a short statement for the press, all the packs were thrown into an Eddie Bauer van and the team went inside the Visitor's Center to order hamburgers and milkshakes and to relax. Once the packs were stowed away in vans and we were seated, the Visitor's Center quieted down and we just looked like another bunch of sunburned climbers who had just been to the top of Rainier.

The climb was successful by a basic standard in mountaineering: the team had returned safely.

In terms of courage, Chuck could measure each step in pain.
The blind could count each dark step over an unseen space.
The deaf could not hear the sound of wind and the roar of avalanches.
Everyone sensed the joy of the summit.

Each of the disabled climbers knew he or she had done something never done before for themselves and for all disabled persons. It was becoming apparent, also, that they had set a standard for even the non-disabled. They had done what most of the non-disabled can only look at or think about. They had overcome their personal mountains of challenge and enjoyed a full experience on one of nature's majestic peaks.

EPILOG

The Pelion team members returned from Mt. Rainier on the 4th of July, Independence Day, and were treated as heroes. During the evening of the 4th, at a salmon bake at Jim Whittaker's home on the shores of Puget Sound, Ted Koppel and his TV crew filmed interviews. These interviews and clips from the media over the previous week became the basis of a full half-hour "Nightline" show.

On July 5th Chuck flew home to meet his new children. Fitz returned home to reconnect with his wife and his new daughter who had been born two weeks before the trip started. The rest of us relaxed.

On July 7th the rest of the Pelion team traveled to Washington, D.C. to meet President Reagan in the Rose Garden the following day. On Wednesday morning, July 8, several of the team appeared on various TV programs. Rich and Judy were on "Good Morning America." Justin and Sheila were on the "Today Show."

Later in the morning there was a private tour of the White House and a reception with the President in the Rose Garden. The President shook hands with each of us. I presented the bag of jelly beans and the American Flag, both of which had been carried to the summit for the

President for his IYDP initiative. He spoke of the courage of the climbers and the spirit they represented.

He said, "When you came down from that mountain it wasn't the experienced leading the disabled; but rather those who could see leading those who could not; those who could hear helping those who could not. The tremendous bond that was forged by this experience, where you complemented each other and joined together to accomplish a great goal, is a significant lesson in what all of us as Americans can accomplish if we work together."

That afternoon Judy, Dusty and I went to the Senate Office Building to hear the Speaker read Senate Resolution No 167, as reported in the July 8, 1981 Congressional Record—Senate, S7263, recognizing the Pelion Project with "—be it Resolved, That the Senate honors and pays tribute to the disabled individuals who climbed Mt. Rainier in the State of Washington, on July 3, 1981, and demonstrated to the World that disability is often a matter of perception."

Pelion was undertaken to provide a demonstration of the capabilities of the disabled. The film that Rick Ridgeway recorded was sold to Home Box Office and made into an award winning film, "To Climb A Mountain." and all the tapes that Doug Wakefield made were edited into a half-hour National Public Radio program called "The Inner Challenge" which is available through NPR.

JULY 4, INDEPENDENCE DAY, PARADISE LODGE

The overwhelming response by the media and the universal cheers from a large number of people signifies that Pelion was more than a statement about the capabilities of people with physical limitations. Pelion was a statement about the human spirit; of courage and adventure.

After returning from the climb all members of the team were asked to speak to numerous groups as individuals, telling their own story, and as groups of two or more. Many talks that I gave were to groups with disabilities and people working with the disabled. The example of Pelion had encouraged them to explore new avenues of activity and to provide greater levels of opportunity and access for persons with disabilities. Each time new opportunities are found because of Pelion, a breath of summit air makes the eagle feathers dance. The medicine of belief and human spirit is offered to the four winds, to the heavens and to mother earth.

CONGRESSIONAL RECORD

JULY 8, 1981

SENATE RESOLUTION NO. 167—COMMENDING THE DISABLED INDIVIDUALS WHO CLIMBED MOUNT RANIER, WASH., DURING THE SUMMER OF 1981

Mr. DOLE. Mr. President, I send a resolution to the desk which I believe would be cosponsored by all Senators if they could be contacted but, as of now, about 70 Members of the Senate are cosponsors. I ask for the immediate consideration of this resolution, and I think it has been cleared with the leadership on both sides.

Mr. ROBERT C. BYRD. Mr. President, will the Senator yield?

Mr. DOLE. I am happy to yield.

Mr. ROBERT C. BYRD. Mr. President, the resolution has been cleared on both sides. There is no objection from the minority to its immediate consideration.

The PRESIDING OFFICER. The resolution will be stated by title.

The legislative clerk read as follows:

A resolution (S. Res. 167) to commend the disabled individuals who climbed Mount Rainier, Washington, during July of 1981.

Mr. DOLE. Mr. President, I wonder if the clerk might read the resolution.

The PRESIDING OFFICER. The clerk will read the resolution.

The legislative clerk read as follows:

S. RES. 167

To commend the disabled individuals who climbed Mount Rainier, Washington, during the summer of 1981.

Whereas nine men and two women braved the perils of nature to climb Mount Rainier in the State of Washington, on July 3, 1981;

Whereas seven of the climbers are blind, two deaf, one an epileptic, and one an amputee;

Whereas the climbers had little or no previous experience in mountain climbing, but all surmounted their disabilities to triumph over the highest mountain in the continental United States;

Whereas a handicapped person is disabled only to the extent that he or she is limited by physical or attitudinal barriers;

Whereas this courageous group of disabled individuals represents a living demonstration of the human capability in Tennyson's words "to strive, to seek, to find, and not to yield"—even against a mountain: and

Whereas this climb deserves to be celebrated throughout this Nation as an act of tremendous courage and inspiration and as a major achievement of the International Year of Disabled Persons: Now, therefore, be it

Resolved, That the Senate honors and pays tribute to the disabled individuals who climbed Mount Rainier in the State of Washington, on July 3, 1981, and demonstrated to the World that disability is often a matter of perception;

SEC. 2. The Secretary of the Senate shall transmit a copy of this resolution to:
Kirk Adams, Snohomish, Washington;
Sheila Holzworth, Des Moines, Iowa;
Dr. Raymond Keith, Arlington, Virginia;
Justin McDevitt, Rosemont, Pennsylvania;
Alec Naiman, New York, N.Y.
Fred Noesner, Glenside, Pennsylvania;
Charles O'Brien, Carlisle, Pennsylvania;
Dr. Judith W. Oehler, Hingham, Massachusetts;
Richard Rose, Vancouver, Washington;
Paul Stefurak, Federal Way, Washington;
Douglas Wakefield, Arlington, Virginia.

Mr. DOLE. Mr. President, I ask unanimous consent that we might hold this resolution at the desk until the close of business. I know there are other Senators who would like to become cosponsors, and I have a list of the cosponsors that I had. I ask unanimous consent that those 70-some Senators be added as cosponsors.

The PRESIDING OFFICER. Without objection, it is so ordered.

The cosponsors of the resolution are as follows:

Mr Stafford, Mr. Jackson, Mr. Weicker, Mr. Randolph, Mr Abdnor, Mr. Andrews, Mr. Armstrong, Mr Baker, Mr. Baucus, Mr. Bentsen, Mr. Boren, Mr Boschwitz, Mr. Burdick, Mr Robert C. Byrd, Mr. Cannon, Mr. Chafee, Mr Cochran, Mr. Cohen, Mr. Cranston, Mr. D'Amato, Mr Danforth, Mr DeConcini, Mr Denton, Mr Durenberger, Mr East, Mr Eagleton, Mr. Ford, Mr Garn, Mr. Glenn, Mr. Gorton, Mr. Hatch, Mr. Hatfield, Mrs. Hawkins, Mr. Hayakawa, Mr. Heinz, Mr. Helms, Mr. Huddleston, Mr. Humphrey, Mr. Johnston, Mrs. Kassebaum, Mr. Kasten, Mr. Kennedy, Mr. Laxalt, Mr. Leahy, Mr. Levin, Mr. Mathias, Mr. Matsunaga, Mr. Mattingly, Mr. McClure, Mr. Metzenbaum, Mr. Mitchell, Mr. Moynihan, Mr. Nickles, Mr. Nunn, Mr. Packwood, Mr. Pell, Mr. Pryor, Mr. Riegle, Mr. Roth, Mr. Sarbanes, Mr. Sasser, Mr. Schmitt, Mr. Specter, Mr. Stennis, Mr. Tsongas, Mr. Thurmond, Mr. Wallop, Mr. Warner, Mr. Williams, and Mr. Zorinsky.

Mr. DOLE. Mr. President, I would just like to take a minute to extend my congratulations. The resolution has been read. I think it is self-explanatory.

This morning this outstanding group had the opportunity to meet with the President of the United States, and he expressed his thanks and admiration. It is very appropriate that such an outstanding performance of people with so-called disabilities should occur during the summer of 1981, which has been declared the International Year of Disabled Persons.

SYMBOLIC CLIMB

As indicated in the resolution, there were nine men and two women, whose names have been referred to, who accomplished this outstanding climb. It just seems to me that it is something we should take note of.

This mountain not only is the highest peak in the continental United States, but it has overcome many more experienced climbers in the past. This mountain represents the ultimate physical barrier to disability, and yet it did not prevent seven blind people, two that were deaf, one an epileptic, and one an amputee, from achieving great heights.

During this International Year of Disabled Persons, there is no more fitting tribute to the potential of handicapped people than to commemorate their tremendous progress in this symbolic climb. They did not pause once to dwell on what they could not do—they set out to prove what they could do, despite what others might call their disabilities. And their spirit has inspired us all.

CONQUERING DISABILITIES

Here in this great country of ours we need more of an active effort to emphasize and utilize the talents of 35 million Americans who happen to be handicapped. They have the confidence and the courage to overcome their limitations—we, as a society need only to remove the physical and attitudinal barriers which continue to remain—we need to welcome them into the mainstream of our communities.

Most Americans cannot boast of the kinds of singular achievement that we are commending here today in the Senate. Their experience shines as a beacon of inspiration to all those who have become discouraged trying to accomplish lesser deeds. They have vividly and unforgettably demonstrated that handicapped people are disabled only to the extent that they are prevented from accomplishment.

CONGRATULATIONS TO INDIVIDUALS

The Senator from Kansas joins his colleagues in commemorating the magnificent victory of 11 individuals over a majestic peak. We are proud of all those who participated in this symbolic climb:

Kirk Adams, Snohomish, Wash.; Sheila Holzworth, Des Moines, Iowa; Dr. Raymond Keith, Arlington, Va.; Justin McDevitt, Rosemont, Pa.; Alec Naiman, New York, N.Y.; Fred Noesner, Glenside, Pa.; Charles O'Brien, Carlisle, Pa.; Dr. Judith W. Oehler, Hingham, Mass.; Richard Rose, Vancouver, Wash.; Paul Stefurak, Federal Way, Wash.; and Douglas Wakefield, Arlington, Va.

We thank them for the shining example that they have set for the rest of us during this special year, and we also pay tribute to those experienced climbers who joined in their effort: Phillip Barton, president of the Institute for Outdoor Awareness, Swarthmore, Pa.; Glenn A. Brindeiro, Renton, Wash.; Timothy Egan, Seattle, Wash.; Dr. Roy Fitzgerald, board member, Institute for Outdoor Awareness, Swarthmore, Pa.; Svein Gilje, Seattle, Wash.; Nancy Gofort, Seattle, Wash.; Don Goodman, Seattle, Wash.; Egil Krogh, Seattle, Wash.; Ray Nichols, Issaquah, Wash.; George S. Niebel, Kirkland, Wash.; Dianne Robert, photographer, Seattle, Wash.; Warren Thompson, Renton, Wash.; and Jim Whittaker, leader of the team, Seattle, Wash.

At this point, it might be appropriate for us to express our appreciation also for the role played by the Institute for Outdoor Awareness, which sponsored this great expedition. We look forward to more such endeavors and thank this nonprofit institute for making this climb possible during the International Year of Disabled Persons. It is an achievement that all Americans will remember for years to come.

I am pleased the leadership, Senator ROBERT C. BYRD and Senator BAKER, have agreed to let us use this unusual procedure to bring the matter to the attention of our colleagues.

I wish to thank Senator JENNINGS RANDOLPH, Senator STAFFORD, Senator WEICKER, Senator JACKSON and the other original cosponsors. It would seem to me that, having had a lot of contact with many who are perceived to have disabilities, this has been a great inspiration to many people in this Nation. I think it will do a great deal in the months and years ahead to better the understanding between people without handicaps and people with so-called handicaps—handicaps that, I believe, are still only in the eye of the beholder.

I suggest that it represents a living demonstration of the human potential, "to strive, to seek, to find, and not to yield"—even against imposing obstacles presented by a great mountain.

If it is satisfactory to the Senator from Connecticut and the Senator from Louisiana, I would like to yield to the Senator from Washington.

The PRESIDING OFFICER. The Senator from Washington.

Mr. GORTON. Mr. President, I should like to thank the distinguished Senator from Kansas and the other prime sponsors for their thoughtfulness in drafting this resolution in the first place and to add my congratulations to the courage and resourcefulness of the climbers themselves.

I can, perhaps, do that a little more fervently than most other Members of this body as I managed to make it to the top of Mount Rainier myself three summers ago in what was, I can assure the other Members, the most physically demanding feat which I have ever accomplished.

As a result, my special admiration goes out to this group, both for the imagination to conceive of this climb, to the great courage and physical strength which they showed in their ability to do so, but, most significantly of all, for what they showed to the people of the United States that can be accomplished by those who are labeled as being physically disabled.

Each one of these individuals overcame what would be considered just a very few years ago an insuperable handicap in making this climb. What they have done is to accomplish a feat of great significance to themselves as individuals but every bit as significantly a feat which will light a beacon for others who are disabled as they are to take on any task whatsoever with a very real chance of success.

Mr. ROBERT C. BYRD addressed the Chair.

The PRESIDING OFFICER. The minority leader is recognized.

Mr. ROBERT C. BYRD. Mr. President, I join with Mr. DOLE in expressing congratulations to this very extraordinary group of individuals who have demonstrated unusual courage and a great deal of determination and resolve. They are to be congratulated.

I am glad to see the Senate extending its recognition to them for having achieved this very unusual and extraordinary goal. They have the kind of faith and courage that certainly are outstanding and should prove to be exemplary to the rest of us as we attempt to surmount lesser obstacles in life.

I thank Mr. DOLE for his thoughtfulness in offering the resolution.

Mr. JOHNSTON. Mr. President, I also join with Senator DOLE, Senator BYRD, and others in congratulating this group. As a coauthor of that resolution, I congratulate the group for their courage.

The PRESIDING OFFICER. The question is on agreeing to the resolution.

The resolution (S. Res. 167) was agreed to.

The preamble was agreed to.

SINCE PELION

I like to think that the offerings on the summit to the four directions, to the heavens and earth spread in distance and time and planted seeds of change and challenge. Since Pelion, individuals with disabilities have climbed the biggest cliffs and the highest mountains.

1990 PEACE CLIMB

Bud Krogh and Warren Thompson, two of the support people, reflected on Pelion's use of a mountain climbing expedition as a social statement and conceived the idea of a climb to support world peace. They thought about a climb of Mt Everest with a team made up of members from the Soviet Union, the People's Republic of China and the United States, the three largest protagonists during the Cold War period. In addition to the summit another objective was to clean up the trash accumulating from years of climbing expeditions. They approached Jim Whittaker and Dianne Roberts with the idea.

Jim is a power house in negotiation skills and Dianne an artful planner. The two of them orchestrated one of the most historic efforts in the stimulation of world peace known as the 1990 Peace Climb. Jim chronicles in his book, *Life On the Edge,* his tireless globe hopping efforts to allow the governments to participate with each other and save political face.

Mt. Rainier was the training ground for the international team members.

On Everest it had been one of the coldest Springs in living memory, capped by the longest period of sustained high winds ever experienced, as the jet stream scoured the upper reaches of Everest continuously for more than 70 days. At one point the winds above the North Col were so strong that a strapping, 250- pound fullback of a climber, carrying a 50-pound load, was literally picked up off his feet by the wind and flown at the end of his safety line like a kite!

Warren wrote to me two stories about events on Everest that reminded him of the Native American Ceremony provided by Joe Washington. He said the news of the winds blowing a climber off his feet had a dramatic effect on the Soviet climbers at Base Camp who were preparing for their forthcoming trek up the mountain to stock Camp 5. They decided they needed something much more fortifying than the standard Base Camp menu would afford. So, they "bribed" the Base Camp jeep driver to make a trip to the nearest village and purchase two sheep.

As the Soviets were about to "dispatch" the hapless sheep in front of the Base Camp cook tent, one of the Chinese (Tibetan) climbers saw what was taking place and sounded the alarm. Instantly, the entire

Chinese team scrambled out of their tents, clamoring about the sacrilege that was about to transpire. They explained, in near panic, that Mount Everest was the "Goddess Mother of the Earth" and that this place, at her very feet, was the Holiest of land. As Buddhists believe that all life is sacred, killing the sheep here would constitute a grievous offense in the presence of the Goddess Mother. They implored the Soviets not to commit this transgression, as the Goddess Mother would surely vent her wrath on the entire expedition with calamitous effect.

Somewhat perplexed by the commotion, the Soviets conceded that they would transport the sheep further down the mountain in the morning to do their "dirty business." The Tibetans happily relinquished the fight and retired to their tents, whereupon the Soviets led the sheep out of sight, behind the cook tent, and promptly killed them.

Within the hour, streams of menacing black clouds tumbled over the ridges surrounding Base Camp, filling the Rongbuk glacier valley from rim to rim. Heavy snow began falling, followed by intense gale-force winds, whipping up a frightful blizzard, knocking down tents and blowing supplies helter-skelter in every direction (some of which were found days later on the valley walls more than a thousand feet above Base). But most frightening of all was the artillery barrage of lightning bolts striking everywhere at once. The first one took out the radio antenna in a deafening, blinding flash.

The storm lasted for three days, and at the exact hour the sheep had been killed, it suddenly dissipated, evaporating into the mists and leaving behind all manner of destruction. Even the upper camps on the mountain had not been spared. The cardinal rule, adopted by unanimous consent of all the citizens of Base Camp, thereafter became, "No more sheep!"

Subsequently, the climb progressed slowly and painfully up the mountain, fighting the incessant jet stream winds on the upper slopes with every step. Jim Whittaker began to worry that a summit bid might not be possible. The last 1000 feet up the summit ridge would be completely exposed and virtually impassable under such conditions.

In an evening satellite phone call to his wife Dianne Roberts, at their home in Port Townsend, Dianne reminded Jim of the spiritual intervention on the Pelion climb. He wondered if Dianne might be able to contact Joe Washington and request a "stop the wind" ceremony. Dianne said she would try.

Dianne found that Joe Washington had passed away two years before. She then called Susan Page and Jake Page, two close friends of Jim and Dianne. Jake had been editor of the Smithsonian Magazine and for several years had been working on projects with southwest Indians. They put Dianne in contact with a spiritual leader on the Navajo reservation. When she stated her request, she was told that the Wind was the most forceful and strong-willed of all the four Elements (Earth, Wind, Fire and Water). "You cannot tell the Wind to stop," he said. "You must appeal to his ego. You must tell him how great and powerful he is. You must express your amazement that he can, so quickly and easily, assert dominion over any place on Earth with his awesome power. And, you must exclaim that even the apex of Earth's domain (Mount Everest) has been humbled by his might, and wonder what will be the next place to experience his indomitable strength." With that, he said he would make such a supplication to the Wind.

The first summit attempt was scheduled for the next day. At sunrise, Everest dawned in clear, azure skies. There was no banner cloud blowing from Everest's summit -- as there had been for every one of the preceding 70 days. The mountain was placid beyond belief. Jim was ebullient. He immediately called Dianne to congratulate her, but as he tried to announce the good news, Dianne interrupted, saying: "Jim! You're going to have to speak louder! There's a tremendous wind storm here. It's knocking down trees and threatening to tear the roof off! I can barely hear you!"

Mt. Everest stayed clear and calm for the next 10 days straight. The expedition placed 21 climbers on the summit, including the first two Soviet climbers to summit without supplemental oxygen, the first Soviet woman to summit Mt. Everest, and the first American to summit solo, without oxygen and setting a new record by ascending directly from Camp 6 to the summit, bypassing Camp 7, and descending all the way down to Camp 5 in a single day. Consequently, the 1990 Mt. Everest Peace Climb is listed in the Guinness Book of World Records as the most successful mountaineering expedition in history.

TRANSCENDENCE

In Warren Thompson's reflections on the descent from Pelion he touched on the transcendent connections between the mountaineer's joy of the summit to non-mountaineers. He experienced another transcendent experience during the Peace Climb.

"While summit preparations were in their final stages, I received a fax (on our satellite communications system) from a Fourth Grade elementary school teacher in Florida. She wrote that her class had been following our expedition for several months and had charted our progress up the mountain on a large drawing of Mt. Everest. She noted that our original objective had been to reach the summit by the 20th anniversary of Earth Day -- the 22nd of April. That date had passed and there had been no news reports from the mountain.

She said that one of her pupils was a young boy named Luke. Luke had been the victim of severe child abuse and had been removed from his parent's custody at the beginning of the school year. Luke had not spoken a single word since that day. That morning, when he came into class, he raised his hand (for the first time during the entire school year) and said, "Do you think they made it?"

I was overwhelmed. My heart ached! I was choked with emotion. I could not believe that climbing a mountain, 10,000 miles away, could have such meaning to him that it would transcend the pain of his trauma. She wanted to know if we could provide her -- and Luke -- with an update. From that day until the end of the expedition, I sent daily updates to her class. At the end of the climb, I sent Luke an expedition poster signed by the entire team, along with this message: "Whatever you dream, you can accomplish!"

"I should have said that if you pursue your dreams, you can accomplish much more than you ever dream possible. I dreamed of putting Americans, Soviets and Chinese climbers together on top of the world's highest peak, to demonstrate what can be accomplished by dedication to a common purpose. What we accomplished was much more than that for an abused child half way around the globe."

ARM POWER

On June 18, 2000, Pete Rieke a paraplegic powered his way to the summit of Rainier using a sled with spiked tractor- like treads called a snowpod. The treads were driven with a rotating arm crank like a bicycle wheel. Pete was paralyzed from the waist down in a rock climbing accident in 1994. Fellow workers and climbing friends helped design and develop his snowpod. They also served as guides, provided support by anchoring ropes for safety and moving the anchors as needed, and assisted in route finding.

TOP WITH NO VIEW

On July 30, 2003 a blind climber, Erik Weihenmeyer made it to the summit of Mt Everest. As in Pelion, the only thing he could not do was see the view.

HISTORY OF MT RAINIER

http://www.americanparknetwork.com/parkinfo/content.asp?catid=85&contenttypeid=30

is a website on the history of Mt Rainer. In the section on *Human History* several events are relevant to Project Pelion

1899: Mount Rainier is established as the nation's fifth national park.

PELION

1962: Mount Rainier is the training ground for the successful American expedition to Mount Everest. (The expedition on which Jim Whittaker became the first American to climb Mount Everest.)

1981: Nine out of 11 members of Project Pelion, a group of climbers with disabilities, reach the summit.

BEFORE PELION
(SOME THINGS ABOUT THE AUTHOR)

Just as Mt Pelion was piled on top of Mt. Ossa and Ossa on top of Mt. Olympus, this Pelion adventure builds on a unique combination of personal experiences. My first mountain was, in fact, Mt. Olympus. When I was in scouting our scout leader took four of us up Mt. Olympus on the Olympic peninsula in Washington. It was a fantastic set of experiences. The next year I was old enough to join the Seattle Mountaineers and took their climbing courses and climbed Rainier via the Emmons route in 1951. I was trained and mentored by people concerned with safety and appreciation of the out-of-doors, trails and peaks.

MOUNT OLYMPUS

As a child I was asthmatic and limited in my sports options. Many nights I watched from my bedroom window while the other kids in the neighborhood played basketball. My interests were books and a chemistry set and model building. My father was foreman in a logging camp when I was born and later owned a log patrol company for saw mills in Puget Sound. In a sense he was like the marshals in the western movies trying to catch the cattle thieves.

Dad protected the logs that would go to the saw mills from log rustlers and small sawmills that scavenged stray drifting logs. Just like cows, logs were branded and tell-tale signs of rustling could be found in the sawed off ends of logs with brands on them drifting down the Duwamish River or in Elliot Bay.

Woods, logging and hunting were in the family tradition. His father left an Indian reservation in northern California when he was only twelve, hiking north into Oregon to find work and a place to help raise his brother. Having Indian blood made me a candidate for being the Indian in games of cowboys and Indians and added a romantic notion to my outdoor experiences.

I found that above timberline I could breathe and exert myself like I never could at home. Once I found a way into the mountains through the Seattle Mountaineers, my life was climbing and studying. I climbed and/or skied most weekends for several years, taught climbing, and was active in mountain rescue activities.

The Mountaineers had rope stations scattered around Seattle. My parents allowed our back porch to serve as one. It was a big box with eight to ten climbing ropes. A mountaineer could check out a rope whenever they needed one. If I was around the house when someone was picking up a rope I would ask where they were going and sometimes, if I could go with them. I always had a climbing pack ready.

The Seattle Mountaineers was a growth experience. Even at the age of fifteen I was teaching climbing, it seemed as an equal, with people several times my age, including, doctors, professors, engineers, postmen and high school dropouts, men and women. The teaching experience was special in that I taught people skills that their lives --and mine-- would depend upon.

MT. OSSA

(I have never climbed M.t Ossa, although there are several. Ossa here, represents a second major set of professional experiences which would lead to Pelion).

My grounding in teaching to foster a supportive team carried over into experiences in industry and academic teaching, first, as faculty member at Northern Arizona University and later at The Wharton School at the University of Pennsylvania, and into consulting activities in industry and government organizations.

Being from Seattle I found my first job after graduating at the Boeing Company. My years there were a continuation in growth working in plasma physics research labs; in the Minuteman Missile System Program Management; and in the research planning department. In 1958 I helped develop the research plan for the company and picked up an MBA trying to figure out what everybody liked about the plan. While I was taking graduate courses I also got into computer programming and system analysis at Boeing.

Coming from undergraduate work in chemistry and physics sciences many of the behavioral courses required in the MBA program made me think more about organizational structure and the concept of a climbing team, goal setting, the setting into process the actions necessary to achieve the goal…the summit.

At first glance the summit as a metaphor for organizational objectives seems blurry because when you get on top of a peak, you have to climb down. The imagery sharpens when one looks at the life cycle of organizations. The demands for organizations and products and services change and everybody has to climb back down into the valleys in order to start a new route up.

While researching concepts on needs and values in shaping behavior in organizations I remembered sitting on a steep, pumice-strewn ridge near the top of Mt Adams a number of years before. Four or five older climbers (thirties was old then) were complaining among themselves about the attitudes of some of the younger climbers (late teens and early twenties) who seemed more oriented to "bagging" a lot of peaks rather than enjoying the scenery and the majesty of the mountains. When I moved nearer the younger group they were carping about the older climbers being too slow. It was a startling realization, for me anyway, that everyone climbing a mountain is climbing it for a different reason and everybody in an organization is there for a different reason.

Years later I was teaching at the University of Pennsylvania Wharton School of Business with an interest in organizational architecture not unlike putting together a climbing team. I happened to talk with a childhood friend who worked in the White House and we talked about organizational concepts. He invited me to come down and look at some issues for him.

BEFORE PELION

The details would require more pages than necessary but a spin-off of the experience was some consulting in the Philadelphia office concerned with drug abuse treatment and prevention. They wanted a course on Management-By-Objectives, a then in-vogue management concept. I suggested I could teach them more about management, communication and team building with one day of rock climbing than I could with a week in a classroom. They split fifty-fifty on wanting to go climbing so we did the classroom exercises. But they wanted to try out climbing as an adjunct to drug treatment. Three teams were organized from participants in drug treatment programs.

After a couple of trips I was encouraged to go after a grant to do a much larger study on the effectiveness of challenge in changing behavior. This led me to the formation of The Institute For Outdoor Awareness, Inc.

The Institute provided outdoor education and challenge trips. Trips were provided for people in a variety of therapy settings, for management training, and teacher training. As described in the first chapter, it was on an Institute outing that the concept of climbing Mt. Rainier was conceived as a way of demonstrating what people can do if they are given a chance.

www.ingramcontent.com/pod-product-compliance
Lightning Source LLC
Chambersburg PA
CBHW080939040426
42444CB00015B/3377